THINGS SEEN AND HEARD

THINGS SEEN AND HEARD

By EDGAR J. GOODSPEED

Essay Index Reprint Series

BOOKS FOR LIBRARIES PRESS
FREEPORT, NEW YORK

First Published 1925
Reprinted 1968

LIBRARY OF CONGRESS CATALOG CARD NUMBER:
68-29208

PRINTED IN THE UNITED STATES OF AMERICA

To
E. B. G.

ACKNOWLEDGMENT

Six of the papers here printed have appeared in the "Atlantic Monthly," and one was printed in the "Chicago Herald." Editorial permission to reprint them in this volume is gratefully acknowledged.

TABLE OF CONTENTS

THINGS SEEN AND HEARD

MY academic orbit is not too rigid to permit an occasional deviation into the outer world. At such times I direct my steps into the neighboring City of Destruction, where, in a lofty building, is one of those centers of light and leading which punctuate the darkness of the metropolis. The structure is not externally remarkable, but the modest fraction of it assigned to my activities is certainly no ordinary apartment.

The extraordinary thing about my classroom is its sides. One is formed by a vast accordion door, loosely fitting, as is the manner of such doors. It faithfully conceals the persons behind it and their every action, while it as faithfully transmits all they may have to say. Theirs is an eloquent concealment. From the sounds that well through the ample interstices of that door, we gather that it is psychology that is going on in the adjoining room. The fascinating affirmations of that most intimate science break in upon our occasional pauses with startling effect. It is thus beyond doubt that theology should always be inculcated; to a psychological obligato, an accompaniment of the study of the mind.

Even more unusual is the other side of the room. From floor to ceiling it is all of plate glass, not meanly divided into little squares, but broadly spaced, so that you are hardly conscious it is there. Through it you may behold, as in an aquarium, a company of men and women going through many motions but making no sound. A tall, romantic youth, presumably the teacher, stands before them, and they rise up and sit down for no perceptible reason and to no apparent purpose. One of them will get up and stand for a long time, and then will as suddenly and causelessly sit down again. At other times, even more distressing, they are all motionless. Lips move, but they give forth no sound. It is like a meeting of the deaf-and-dumb society. Worst of all, they will sometimes unanimously and quite without warning rise in their places, simultaneously adjust their wraps, and silently depart. It is as if they all suddenly realized that they have had enough of it. You know that you have. There is something weird in all this soundless action, this patient, motiveless, mechanical down-sitting and uprising, something far more distracting even than in those disembodied psychological voices that murmur in our ears.

But much more disturbing than either of these extraordinary neighbors of our reflections is their combination. The sounds that come through the door do not tally with the sights that come through the glass. What you hear bears no relation to what you see. It does not even contradict it. There is a war in your members. Your senses do not agree.

And yet you are haunted by the notion that what you are hearing has something to do with what you are seeing. When someone asks a question behind the door at your left

[3]

and someone makes a motion beyond the glass at your right, you instinctively try to relate the two. But in vain; there is no relation. Especially when all the visibles get up and leave, it seems as if it must be because of something the audibles have said. Nevertheless, the audibles go right on psychologizing, entirely oblivious of the visibles' departure.

Reflection has satisfied me that much confusion of the modern mind is due to the incongruity of what we hear and what we see. The conditions of my quaint lecture-room are typical. You look about upon a community of earnest, hard-working people, soberly doing their daily work at business and at home. But you pick up the home edition and read of a very different world of violence and vice. All its men are scoundrels and its women quite different from those you see, to say the least. You have long been assured that this is the Age of Reason; but observation finds little to support the claim. The Age of Impulse would seem as good a guess. You hear that the League of Nations is dead, but on

visiting the movies you are astonished to see
it in session and to find that it yet speaketh.
You are told on all hands that everything
about the war was a failure, and yet, as a
whole, it seems to have accomplished its
immediate end. You hear much lamentation
over the sensationalism of the press, but as
you read it, it is its conventionality that of-
tener leaves you mourning. The newspapers
show you a comfortable view of the steel
strike, but the cook's brother, who was one
of the strikers, tells you something entirely
different. With a laudable desire to preserve
your reason, you do your best to cultivate the
virtues of blindness, deafness, insensibility,
and unbelief. Yet you are sometimes just a
little bewildered. Your universe is not uni-
fied.

The most disturbing thing is not that
things seen and things heard contradict each
other: that we might learn to allow for. The
great trouble is that they seem to bear no relation to each other at all. Most political
talk is of this description. It has nothing to

do with the case. It is like the effort of a young friend of mine who, on being asked to translate a well-known passage of Epictetus, produced the following: "If teachings are no longer the reasons of all things, and who has false doctrines, how much should be the cause, and as such the destruction."

That mythical creature, the American of British fiction, so boldly portrayed by Mr. Chesterton, Mr. Buchan, Mr. Oppenheim, and Mr. Doyle, much as we love and enjoy him, is, it must be confessed, little known save by reputation on this side of the sea. He is fiction in the strictest sense. Like Mr. De Quincey's unfortunate reporter, *non est inventus*. But he is not the less popular among us for being an imported article. He is so rich, so ready, so unspoiled, so clear-eyed, clean-limbed, nasal-toned, poker-faced, and, best of all (true to the great traditions of his country), so quick on the trigger!

The trouble is not merely that the things we hear we never see, but that the things we see we never hear. For how extraordinary is the sensation when you hear of something you have seen! Perhaps it is only an accident. Do you not yearn to rise up and cry out, "I saw that! I was there"? It is because, for once, things seen coincide with things heard.

Brain-proud men of science sourly say that Greek is dead. But to the Grecian mind it is refreshing to observe that familiarity with Greek is now extraordinarily widespread in this country. This is all the more fascinating at a time when the practical educators have triumphantly excluded the study of Greek from most institutions of learning as an impractical subject, not suited to the training of a materialistic people.

As I look about the world in which I live, I observe that every high-school boy or girl knows his Greek letters. He does not have to be compelled to learn them. He wishes to learn them. He would feel humiliated if he did not learn them. He would be looked down upon by his companions as a person without social ideals. His college brothers are equally conversant with the eponym of all alphabets. So are their sisters and their sweethearts. They may not know the rule of three or the multiplication table; they may be without a single formula of chemistry or a solitary principle of physics; but, rely upon it, they will know their Greek letters. Their parents will know them, too. They will learn them at their children's knee, in all docility and eagerness, for fear of disgracing themselves and their offspring by not always and everywhere distinguishing the illustrious Tau Omicron Pi's from the despised Nu Upsilon Tau's. The fact is, it is difficult to be even a successful delivery boy in our community without knowing one's Greek letters.

I doubt whether the Greek alphabet was ever more widely and favorably known than now. In our midst the celebrated Cato could not have survived till eighty without learning it.

I shudder to think what anguish this must cause the practical educators aforesaid, as they walk abroad and see every house boldly and even brazenly labeled with the hated letters. Even their own favorite students, who show promise in the use of test tubes and microscopes, insist upon labeling themselves with more of the Greek alphabet. Why will they not be content to call their honor societies by some practical Anglo-Saxon name, like the Bread and Brick Club, or the Gas and Gavel? But no! These rational considerations have no force with our youth. Nothing will satisfy them but more Greek letters. I have seen a man use twelve of them, or just half the alphabet, to set forth his social and learned affiliations.

Of course, to us Greek professors, shambling aimlessly about the streets with nothing to do, these brass signs are like the faces of old friends (no offense, I hope), and remind us of the names of the books of Homer, if nothing more.

But the Greek renaissance has gone much further than the alphabet. It pervades science. It is positively nonplusing to hear one's scientific friends rambling on in the language of Aristotle and Euclid, with their atoms and ions, their cryoscopes and cephalalgias, their sepsis, diagnosis, and autopsies. The fact is, they really talk very little but Greek, which is one reason why we all admire them so. They are greatest when they are most Greek; and were their Greek vocabulary suddenly taken from them, half their books would shrivel into verbs. Three-fourths of them are indeed teaching Greek as hard as they can, though mercifully unconscious of the fact.

The Greek, on seeing a queer animal, waited until it was dead and then counted its toes. He thus soon knew enough to make a distinction between genus and species, which zoölogists are still talking about. Whence it comes about that our little Greek friends, the lion, the elephant, the rhinoceros, and the hippopotamus, are household favorites still. Consistent people who object to Greek will expunge these words from their vocabulary.

The Greek conquest of our social youth

and of our grizzled age is nothing, however, to its triumphs in commerce. Here both letters and vocabulary come into their own. It must be admitted that we English-speaking people are poor word-makers. Only in moments of rare inspiration do we achieve a Nabisco or a Mazola. But in this age of new creations one of Adam's chief needs is names for the bewildering things he sees about him. How indispensable to us inarticulate moderns is the voluble Greek! Like one who hides a thimble for you to find, he has named everything in advance, and all we have to do is to discover it. From Alpha Beer to Omega Oil, from Antikamnia to Sozodont, the Greek has taught us names. Even automobile is half Greek, which is really what makes it desirable. Who would want an ipso-mobile? And Solon and moron, those twin pillars of the journalistic vocabulary, without which no newspaper could exist a week, are pure Grecian. When I attend the funeral of Greek, therefore, as I am constantly invited to do, I am comforted to observe old Greek himself and his whole family, thinly disguised, heading the chief mourners.

Nowhere is the contrast between things seen and things heard more striking than in language. Very conscientious people have observed this and, fearful of seeming something other than they are, have evolved phonetic spelling. Witty people like Max Beerbohm and Josh Billings have observed it too, and made such use of it as "Yures til deth," and " 'The laibrer iz werthi ov hiz hire,' an that iz aul." Children are proficient here. One I know recently addressed a letter to his "Dere ant LN." "Nit mittenz ar the kynd," as they spell at Lake Placid. An intelligent-looking man steps in front of you at the club and murmurs a deferential "Skewmy," to which you suavely reply, "Doughmeshnit." No one has ever been able to reproduce conversation in print. The gulf between the words we see and the words we say is too great. Feeble efforts in this direction are sometimes made by ambitious writers, but the truth is that, from the standpoint of the printed page, we all speak in dialect.

The fact is, almost everything we hear is more or less conventionalized in type or in telling. People exchange fragments of news, or funny stories of a few familiar types. Newspaper items can easily be grouped under five or six thoroughly conventional heads. An observant friend once remarked that the women of literature were mere pallid contrivances compared to the actual ones we know, and I was really startled to perceive that he was right. Even in books no one will go to the pains of relating things as unconventionally as they really happen. We are accustomed to stereotypes, and we expect and desire them. In reality, of course, things happen much more intricately than anyone will bother to report them, or to hear them reported. This is probably what is meant when we say that truth is stranger than fiction. It is vastly more complex.

Take a simple example. As you plod homeward of an autumn morning, fatigued by the labors of the professorial day, you are met by a colleague of high degree who declares that he has been looking for you. Will you go and meet the Cardinal? Like the Sage of Concord, you like a church, you like a cowl, and you are careful not to say "No," as you conceal your gratification and fence for more definite information. You fortify yourself by the reflection that you have encountered cardinals and dukes before this, and struggle to remember which is His Eminence and which His Grace. It seems that the Archbishop is to bring the Cardinal out from the other end of town, and at one-fifteen they will hesitate at a certain downtown corner long enough to pick you up. All you have to do is to carry your cap and gown, to mark you off from the passing throng. And you would better give the motor-cycle man who will lead the way a memorandum of the route he is to follow.

You do not decline. You move on homeward, thinking quite without effort of some flattering things you will say to the Archbishop and some observations you will address to the Cardinal. In particular, you decide to ask him if, when the German Cardinal condescendingly remarked, "We will not speak of war," he really did answer, "We will not speak of peace." Your simple preparations are soon made, and you make your way downtown in some preoccupation.

Promptness has been said to be the courtesy of princes and you do not wish to disappoint a Prince of the Church. At one-five you take your stand at the curb beside the streaming boulevard. Traffic is at its highest. You are less inconspicuous than you could wish, for no one else is carrying an academic cap in his hand and a doctor's gown upon his arm. But to conceal these accouterments may defeat the purpose of your vigil. It is precisely by a wave of that Oxford cap that you are to bring the whole proud, sacerdotal cortège, motor-cycles and all, to a stop. You scan each south-bound car with eagerness. It becomes one-fifteen. The Archbishop is the soul of promptitude. He should be almost here. You perceive approaching a particularly stately limousine, which conforms to your preconceived ideas of the archiepiscopal in automobiles. It proves to be empty. You have now scanned hundreds of passing cars. It is one-twenty — one-twenty-five — one-thirty. Great heavens! Have you missed the Cardinal's car, Archbishop and all? Even in your dawning dismay habits of scientific observation reassert themselves. The stately limousine you had once taken for his reappears, from the same direction as before and still empty. You are not mistaken. You recognize the chauffeur. You almost think he recognizes you. It strikes you that these cars that you have been seeing are not all different ones, but are simply circling about before you, like Caesar's army on the stage.

It is two o'clock. You despair. The party has eluded you. It has probably already arrived at the University, having gone out some other way. After all, why should you have escorted the Cardinal out? He is escorted everywhere by two archbishops, five motor-cops, five plain-clothes men, and a civilian guard of honor. This should suffice. He is, indeed, a stranger in the city, but he can hardly go astray. You begin to feel sadly superfluous, yet, following a Casabiancan instinct, you stay on. A friend who has observed your situation goes into the club and telephones. He returns to inform you that, owing to the Cardinal's fatigue, the program has been postponed one hour. It is two-ten. You observe that it is just time for him now to be appearing. The stately and mysterious limousine, already twice seen, now passes for the third time. It is still vacant.

The mystery of it fascinates you. Is it inextricably caught in the circling current, like some Flying Dutchman on wheels, powerless to make a port? It occurs to you that, if the cars before you are in some instances merely running around in circles, the foot-passengers behind you may be doing the same thing. Two-twenty-five, and again that silent, vacant, funereal limousine sweeps by, for the fourth time. It is getting on your nerves. Is it possible that public-spirited owners send their limousines on idle afternoons to circle showily about the Avenue, hour after hour, to swell the concourse and thus contribute their mite, as it were, to the gaiety of nations? Or is this mysterious vehicle, with its hawklike circling, bent on some sinister errand of abduction, or worse?

But at this instant a police-gong clangs down the thronging street. Five motor-cops appear, and in the car behind them a medieval saint, a modern archbishop, and divers celebrities such as one sees in guards of honor. One knows them instinctively by their tall hats, and observes that there are still occasions for such hats—the cardinal points of existence, as it were. But you have scarcely registered this observation and handed the leading motor-policeman his typewritten instructions, when you are aware that one of the hats is pointing you to the second car. You turn swiftly to it. The gentlemen in it spring out with surprising agility and make a place for you among them. The cortège has hardly stopped. The nimble gentlemen spring in again (the car is an open one), and you are off.

You experience a momentary disappointment that you are not to hobnob with the illustrious prelates, but bend your attention upon their distinguished representatives about you. They are little given to conversation. If they are not communicative, neither are they inquisitive. They are of a negative demeanor. They drive at a frightful speed, shepherding all other traffic to the curb out of their way as they advance. They achieve this flattering effect by blowing a siren, sounding a loud gong, and hurling deep-throated objurgations, much deeper than you are accustomed to, at anyone who crosses their path. Who are these supreme autocrats, you ask yourself? Mere money could not behave thus. A suspicion crosses your mind, and you ask what car this is. You are informed that it is the Police Car!

Of course, you do in the end meet the Cardinal and set his feet upon the long carpet pontifically stretched for his reception. That is all there is to be said about it. You did meet the Cardinal, and you "acted" (admirable word!) as his escort. But as you look back upon that day, that bald statement does not summarize or even adumbrate its impressions.

In one respect alone that I detect does observation agree with rumor. Both are generally inconclusive. Someone has recently remarked how frequently one who reads is told the beginnings of things and left to conjecture the end. It is just as true of life. We are always wondering what "finally" became of this man and that, once of our acquaintance, and of this movement or that, once brought to our ears. Life and print are alike full of mysterious fragments, which we have not time to fit into their exact places in the general order.

Domestic rearrangements drove me, on a recent winter night, to go to rest in a room at the back of the house, overlooking what I call the garden. Before retiring I put up a window, so that a refreshing whiff of the Stockyards might perfume my dreams and reassure me that there was no immediate danger of famine.

The night was cold, and my efforts at slumber were frustrated by a strange, steadily recurring sound like a man shoveling coal or clearing frozen slush from a sidewalk. But the hour, between eleven and twelve, seemed an improbable time for such operations. About midnight, however, it ceased and I fell asleep.

The next morning I mentioned the sound to a member of the family who had also been sleeping on the garden side of the house, and she declared that she, too, had noticed it and been much mystified about it. It did not seem a reasonable time to shovel off the hardened snow—for it was, of course, hardest at night, when the thermometer was low. What was my astonishment, however, when I retired on the following night, to hear the same harsh, grating sound patiently repeated for an hour or two toward midnight. I thought again of the possibility that it was coal that was being shoveled. Perhaps some poor, unfortunate neighbor was hoarding coal, and his enjoyment took the form of shoveling his hoard over and over, and gloating over it through the midnight hours. This theory appealed to me strongly as I lay awake and listened to the sound, until I noticed that the shoveled stuff, whatever it was, made no sound when it fell. It therefore could not be coal.

It must, of course, be snow, or at least must fall upon a bed of snow, which made it noiseless. But why this tireless shoveling of hardened snow from the concrete walks night after night in the dead vast and middle of the night? Was it some wretch who had formerly neglected his sidewalks and so wrought an involuntary homicide, who now, sleepless with remorse, must pick away with ringing shovel at the icy crust till midnight came to his relief? I never learned. Should these lines ever meet the eye of an elderly seafaring man, a pigeon-tamer by trade, who called upon me last Saturday on his way home to Pittsburgh from his second mother-in-law's funeral five miles from Madison, Wisconsin, which he had attended because he considered a wife the best friend a man has in the world, and his second wife, with whom he had become acquainted through advancing her eight dollars to enable her to reach Pittsburgh, was one whom he could not surpass if he married a thousand times; but in returning from which to Chicago by train, overcome by grief and fatigue, he had been robbed of all his money except fourteen dollars and was forced in consequence to seek out his old employer, a professor variously pronounced Riddle, Griggle, and Gridley, but spelled Lelley, in default of finding whom or the grand master of his fraternal order in Englewood, he was reduced to borrowing enough money to make up the price of a ticket to Pittsburgh, or four dollars and eighty-seven cents, from me, a perfect stranger—I should be glad to hear from him again. Until when, I shall continue to reflect on the disparity of what I have seen with what I have heard. Perhaps he was an actor out of work. If so, the performance was worth something, and it certainly had a plot.

THE LIFE OF ADVENTURE

"ADVENTURES," said the gifted Mr. Disraeli, "are to the adventurous." Stevenson somewhere recommends the conception of life as a series of adventures, each morning witnessing, as it were, a new embarkation upon some treasure-quest or feat of arms. And I have often observed that my adventurous friends have a knack of reporting, with all the flavor of genuine adventures, experiences which upon sober reflection seem rather to fade into the light of common day. It would therefore appear that it is they who put the adventurous into life, rather than life which is responsible.

In this fact lies much encouragement for one whose life seems set in a routine of commonplace; who lives upon a decent city street, where even burglars seldom penetrate, and nothing more exciting than automobile collisions ordinarily happens. These last are, however, of a gratifying frequency, if it is excitement that one craves. Indeed, we have latterly come to a weary sense of annoyance when the familiar crunch informs us that two motorists have simultaneously claimed the right of way. The pious duty of sweeping up all that was mortal of these unfortunates sometimes becomes really distressing, and one feels like a modern Tobit, keeping watch o'er man's mortality.

I make it a point never to witness these distressing occurrences; that would be a vocation in itself. Only when the fatal crash is heard do I emerge, like Aesculapius from his temple. I was a witness once, but only in a burglary. I had not, of course, seen the burglary, but I could remember seeing the *corpus delicti in situ*, as it were, later than anyone else; and the proof that the object had existed had, of course, to precede the evidence that it had disappeared. Such is the logic of the law. Twenty several times I accordingly visited the halls of justice, and twenty several mornings I sacrificed upon the altar of duty. Months wore on; we witnesses, from our frequent meetings, came to be firm friends. We talked of forming a permanent organization. We even began to produce a literature, though all I now remember of it is, "For we're trying Johnny Artzle in the morning."

I became so seasoned an habitué of the court building that belated witnesses for other tribunals, on reaching the witness-room, would rush up to me and explain in broken English that they had been detained, that they had come as fast as they could and hoped I would excuse them; showing that there was nothing about me that looked out of place in the precincts of the Criminal Court.

But, with all this assiduity, we did not convict our burglar. The kindly judge reduced his bail, that he might rejoin his family; he seized the opportunity to filch some golden teeth, which a prosperous dentist had destined for his fashionable clients, and this irate gentleman thrust in his case ahead of ours (though the Statute of Limitations had not yet run against us) and thus snatched from us the satisfaction of immuring our defendant in his deserved dungeon.

This is why I never witness motor accidents. But it is plain that even this unhappy business may take on the glamor of romance when approached from the point of view of adventure. The other morning, when the well-known sound informed us that we were again to function as first aids to broken humanity, I rushed into the street, to see a large limousine of the eight-passenger type now usual at obsequies resting comfortably on its port side on the opposite parkway. What might it not contain, in the way of youth, beauty, and interest? Yet in point of fact, when its cargo had been laboriously hoisted up through the main hatch, which was ordinarily its right-hand door, it proved to be nothing very romantic after all, and we gave it its coffee with a certain vague sense of disappointment. Some people really are not worthy of adventure, and it is a great pity that many who have adventures refuse to accept them gratefully in an adventurous spirit.

War is, of course, the main avenue to adventure, and even so commonplace an affair as military drill has, at least in its early stages, adventurous possibilities. Our corporal (for I have to admit that I am only a private—as yet) being one day kept from duty by a seminar on Plato, an expert on the History of Art, excluding that of war, was set over us. His eagerness exceeded his experience, and it is not too much to say that he led us into places of danger previously unsuspected. The company, though with the gravest misgivings, was called upon to deploy as skirmishers, guide left. Placing himself at our head and crying, "Follow me," our gallant leader at once set off at a double-quick in the wrong direction, where a lieutenant much out of breath overtook us, crying, "Hey, corporal! You belong at the other end of the line!" "Follow me!" ordered our leader unabashed; and we double-quicked to the other end, there to meet the other lieutenant, with the cry, "Hey, corporal! You belong in the middle of the line!"

But one of our most inflexible deans occupied the middle with his squad, and his conception of military duty would not permit him to budge without orders. Perhaps he remembered the Marne and defeat by dislocation. With no place to go, our embarrassment was relieved by the captain's "As you were," and we formed again in our familiar column of squads. But in the slight confusion which I have to admit had for a moment prevailed, a metathesis had taken place: from being third squad we had become fourth, which position carried with it the responsibility of leading the second platoon. When, therefore, the hoarse order, "Platoons column left," rang out, the company plodded placidly on in column of squads. We seemed to have lost our platoon consciousness. Our captain was annoyed; he knew that he had two platoons, but they declined to separate. Again the order came, without effect.

The company now vaguely felt that something was wrong, and suppressed cries of "Hey, corporal! you're pivot man!" "Hey, second platoon! wake up!" came to us from front and rear. With a start, our guilty squad awoke to its new responsibilities, and a sense of the eternal watchfulness of the soldier's life. *Qui vive? Qui va?*

The day before Marshal Joffre arrived, I asked our guide, a Plattsburg veteran, whether the Faculty Company was to participate in his review of the battalion. His face darkened with apprehension.

"Say," said he, "that would be a mess! He's reviewed better troops than we are!"

Never more desperate ones, though, we agreed. Like all great soldiers, our officers are modest, even about their handiwork. We of the ranks, however, in our eagerness feel some disappointment that we cannot exhibit our newly won proficiency, even to General Barry. Why keep it all for Hindenburg?

Battalion drill is a great day in the life of the military neophyte, and our favorite evolution is the company front double-quick. It would have been a pleasure to perform this for the Marshal of France, but our last execution of the maneuver made our officers reluctant to exhibit our proficiency in it again to the jealous eye of authority. In company front, we spread in two ranks well across the field, and at the command "Double time!" we inaugurated a really imposing movement before the reviewing officer. For some reason the front rank of the first squad set a rapid pace, which the whole rank nobly strove to imitate. The second rank, in fear of being distanced, came thundering up behind, and the first rank, hearing their onset close upon their heels, regularly ran away. In consequence, our alignment, usually so precise, suffered considerably; and it began to look like an interscholastic quarter-mile badly bunched at the finish. Reduced to the more professorial "quick time" at the end of the race, we soon recovered our breath if not our composure, and it was remarked that in the rush it had been the Faculty orators that led the field; both things being after all at bottom a matter of wind.

Before we were dismissed that morning, the reviewing officer commented favorably on our drill, excepting only the double-quick, and admonished us to try to keep from laughing. Yet is it not well known from the writings of Captain Beith and others that the British Tommies go into action laughing, joking, and singing music-hall ballads?

The other day the major's usual stirring lecture on the art of war was replaced by that threadbare faculty device, a written quiz. The first question (I believe I am disclosing no military secret in telling) was, "Name the textbook." The answer was, of course, I.D.R.; but some poor fellows who had plunged into the contents without first mastering the cover, were found wanting.

The sociability characteristic of Convocation processions naturally tends to pervade our military marching as well. At battalion the other day we were trying to catch the captain's far-off orders and then to distinguish which of several whistles was the "command of execution" for our company, when a late arrival dropped into the vacant file beside me, and in the most sociable manner began to relate an experience on the rifle range the Saturday before. This extended narrative was much interrupted, for I lost him every little while under the stress of those far-off orders, of which he appeared quite unconscious. His method seemed to be to wait for the evolution to be completed and then rejoin me wherever I might be and resume his parable, though he did occasionally complain that he had not heard the order.

Nevertheless, we learn quickly. The other day the first sergeant, a theologian of a wholly unsuspected bellicosity, called upon the squad leaders to report. The first corporal at once glibly cried out, "All present or accounted for"; whereupon each successive corporal, confident that none of his men had been killed or captured since the day before joyfully answered with the same crisp and comprehensive formula.

For all our attempts at militarism, a certain democratic informality still lingers among us. The captain is ordinarily affectionately addressed as "Henry." Thus while at rest a voice is heard from the rear rank: "Well, Henry, I don't understand what the rear rank is to do on the order, 'Company platoons right.' Now the front rank—"

"There's no such command," answers the captain patiently, thus closing the incident.

The captain frequently marches backward, so that he can face us and enjoy the swift precision with which we carry out his orders. The other day he backed into the east bleacher and sat down abruptly on the bottom step. Fortunately he gave the command to halt, or in our blind obedience we should probably have marched right over him up the bleacher and off the back of it into space.

I shall never forget our first review. It

was with no little reluctance that our captain consented to our participation in it. He seemed to fear that we might shy at the visiting officers' decorations, and run away. Only the most protracted good behavior on our part carried the day. After marching past the reviewing party, in as straight a company front as we could exhibit, we opened our ranks for inspection, and the visiting colonel prowled about among us. Just before he reached our company, a student major, in a frenzy of apprehension, came up and gave us one final adjuration not to wiggle.

The colonel—a fine military figure—marched swiftly up and down our ranks, stopping now and then to address a few crisp questions to one or another of the men. He seemed to select those whose soldierly bearing suggested military promise; at least our corporal and I thought so, as we were the men he spoke to in our part of the line. Or it may be that we were standing so like statues that he wanted to satisfy himself that those marble lips could speak. Our comrades were of course eager to know what he had said, and we had later to tell them that he had imparted to us important military information of a confidential character; to which they cynically replied, "Yaas, he did!"

We also tactfully let it be known that the colonel was anxious to learn whether our officers were perfectly satisfactory. With more tractable and appreciative inquirers we entered into more detail. He had asked the corporal whether he had ever shot a rifle; corporal blushingly admitted that he had once shot a squirrel. (Corporal is a football hero, and accustomed to meet the enemy at much closer quarters than rifle range. The rest of us, on the other hand, are publicists, and are deadliest at distances of from 500 to 5,000 miles.) Number 2 was asked if he could cook, and claimed that he could. Colonel in his haste did not think to ask Number 2 if anyone could eat what he cooked, or he would have learned that Number 2's cookery is best suited to prisoners of war.

Colonel had no sooner departed on his in-

quisitorial way than the student major re-
appeared from nowhere, in a fearful rage, to
inquire if we couldn't stand still even for two
minutes, and to complain bitterly that during
the inspection one man had been guilty of
rubbing his nose. Murmurs of disapproval
ran through the ranks at the mention of this
wretched offender, who was probably responsible for dragging our company down to
a tie with the Law School for third place out
of nine in the honors of the day.

Captain now mercifully ordered, "Rest,"
and a prodigious and concerted sigh rose
from the ranks. Each man abandoned his
poker-like pose of " 'Ten-*shun*" for an attitude of infinite dejection and fatigue. It was
six-fifteen, and I remarked to Number 2 that
my back ached. He said his ached clear
through. Our former corporal asked the captain what a man was to do if he had a dinner
engagement. Captain said he had one, but
guessed we'd all have to wait for orders to
dismiss. Corporal replied that he hadn't one,
but just wanted to know. If one is to rise in

the service, one should never lose an opportunity of extracting military information from one's officers.

We have not yet been promoted to uniforms, but last night after drill we were informed that while we could not be provided with the invisible olive-gray now in fashion, some antiquated khaki-colored uniforms of 1910 were being provided for our adornment. This arrangement met with no objection. The fact is, we are not wholly unaccustomed to wearing clothes of the fashion of 1910, and furthermore, while we have no desire to be conspicuous, some of us rather shrink from the idea of wearing invisible clothing, no matter how fashionable.

So full of adventure is military life, even in its most elementary form. But after all I am not primarily a soldier: I am a human coral insect—that is to say, a university professor, before whom life stretches, as Stevenson said of another class, "long and straight and dusty to the grave." I should like to be a volcanic being, shouldering up whole islands at a heave; or even, if that could not be, perhaps engulfing one or two, reluctantly of course, now and then. Whereas it is my lot in life to labor long and obscurely beneath the surface, to make the intellectual or historical structure of the universe solider by some infinitesimal increment, about which in itself nobody except my wife and me particularly cares.

Sometimes, however, I repine a little and wish I were, say, a porpoise, splashing gaily along at the surface, and making a noise in the world. Once in a while, when I am going to sleep (for even a coral insect must sometimes sleep), dreams float through my mind of sudden achievement, such as might make one a porpoise or better; and once one of these nearly came true. Judge how nearly. I was wandering through a half-subterranean Spanish chapel, fitly set with huge old missals, dark altar-pieces, covered stalls, and quaint curios. Its dim recesses beckoned us on from one rich relic to another. Interest quickened. It seemed a place where anything might be, awaiting only the expert eye of discovery. I had often fancied such a place, and finding in some dim corner of it a certain long-lost work of literature still remembered after a thousand years' absence; somewhere in such a sleepy treasure-house it doubtless lay, enfolding within its moldering folios, not its quaint contents only, but fame and fortune for its finder. And look! Yonder, under a corner staircase, is a shelf of old books, large and small. You approach it with feigned indifference; here, if anywhere, will be your prize, a manuscript whose unique rarity will awaken two hemispheres. It is not among the ponderous tomes, of course; so you take them down first, postponing putting fortune to the decisive touch. But these small octavos have just the look of promise; they are thin, too, as it would be; and what period more likely for it than that sixteenth century to which they so obviously belong?

Only the other day, a friend of mine who lives on our reef, and on a branch even more recondite than mine, found among the un-catalogued antiques of an American museum the one long-lost Tel-el-Amarna tablet, which had disappeared almost as soon as it was discovered, and of which it was only known that it was probably in America. Thus may one be changed in a moment from polyp to porpoise, and be translated from the misty obscurity of the bottom to the stirring, dazzling, delightful surface of things.

But after all, the plain truth is that adventure consists less in the experiences one actually has than in the indefatigable expectancy with which one awaits them. Indeed, I sometimes fear that people must be divided into those who have adventures and those who appreciate them. And between the two the affinity for adventure is greater treasure than the experiencing of it. If we are possessed of the affinity, adventure itself is, at most, just around the corner from us. This opens the life of adventure to all who crave it. What possibilities lie in merely crossing a street, for example! Someone remarked the other day as he dodged across among the motor-cars, "Why not take a chance now and then and lead a real life for a few minutes?"

I therefore recommend the life of adventure. It conceives each day as a fresh enterprise, full of delightful possibilities and promise, and so preserves the wine of life from growing flat.

Here is the secret of youth. The moral of Mr. Disraeli's epigram is, "Be adventurous."

DO ONE AND ONE MAKE TWO?

IT is now, doubtless, too late to hope, even by our improved historical methods, to recover the name of the clever individual who, perhaps in the Stone Age or earlier, arrived at the principle that one and one make two. It is evidently too late to correct him, or even to blame him adequately; and with a handicap of seventy or more centuries, one can hardly hope to undo the mischief he has done. Yet futile as the effort may prove, it is the purpose of these paragraphs to point out the shallow and delusive character of this hoary axiom, and the precarious nature of most of what has been built upon it.

Our cave-dweller Newton may have based his epoch-making equation upon that even more erroneous formula, "One equals one," which had doubtless been invented—I will not say discovered—ages before his time. If not, he could have arrived at it by the simple device of subtracting one from each side of his own discovery—an easy achievement for a mind so original and profound as his. Such a performance, indeed, assumes its result before arriving at it; but that is true of not a few of our most logical processes. And it may be true, speaking quite abstractly, that one equals one. That is, one wholly imaginary unit, of a given size and sort, equals one just such unit, of just such a sort and size, under identical conditions. This is what the mathematicians mean. It is only just to them to say so. The danger is that one will forget that one is playing with imaginary values and try to deal with real units on this principle. The cavern professor can have made no such blunder. He knew that one wife was not equal to another, or one weapon to another, or one enemy to another. If he did not know this, his life was neither long nor happy.

Not that his formula had not a certain limited value. It might help him to keep count of his game, his children, or his day's journeys. But it had no such value as it claimed. It was too broadly and loosely put. Even now, when men have been trying for millenniums to believe in it and make it true, its range of valid applicability is still very limited. For it carries with it a fictitious standardization of units, which breeds a host of misconceptions. In fact, it is precisely as one reduces the application of this equation to narrower and narrower limits that one attains wisdom, culture, and character.

Scarcely had I reached this point in my reflections, when the porter came to remind me that the time changed at Buffalo, and that, if I wished to wake at seven, I must do so at six. So false is it that six and one make seven. But, of course, the equation is valid only if one remains stationary. It is a survival from man's immobile, semi-vegetable period.

I was confiding these heresies to a skeptical friend, as we were passing a potato field. He challenged me at once: Did not one potato and one potato make two potatoes? But suppose one potato to be sweet and sound and large, and the other to be small and wilted and Irish. They are numerically, indeed, two potatoes, but only for arithmetical, not for culinary, purposes. And who cares for the arithmetical value of a potato?

But if one and one make two, we have at once to ask, Two what? Two of whatever one is, doubtless. But which one? This is the heart of the error. One acre plus one acre makes two acres. But suppose one acre is the Isola Bella and the other is selected from the Île du Diable. Or buildings. The Pennsylvania station and the Philadelphia city hall make two—large buildings. This forgets that one exhibits genius as well as magnitude. Or statues: the Adams monument and the Bacchante—two statues certainly, perhaps two masterpieces; but that is not all, or even half. The things are incommensurable, and the sum total is a delusion. It has no meaning or worth unless we are counting pieces for museum vigilance, or in preparation for shipment.

Even money, the final type of standardized unit evolved by our race in a last convulsive effort to make the old adage true, for all its failures—even money is not equal to the task. There is a man in California (of course he would be in California) who has to go every quarter to the bank and deposit a dividend of three hundred and fifty dollars, because once, to help a friend, he put five hundred dollars into that friend's mine. Is the five hundred dollars I lost when my bank failed some years ago equal to his five hundred, and how much are they together? Yet my dollars were just as real and just as numerous as his. There was another five hundred dollars which was not in the bank but long since invested in another mine. Yet that sum in mining stock never sends me toiling to the bank to deposit a quarterly dividend of three hundred and fifty dollars. Indeed, it does not function in my daily life at all, ex-

cept to illustrate poignantly the disparity of
dollars and of mining stocks.

But financiers will say that this is com-
paring dead dollars with living ones. Then
let us deal fairly with both. Does the first
five dollars I earned for teaching (tutoring a
fellow-student in Assyrian, may heaven for-
give me!) only equal the five dollars the bank
occasionally allows me on an abandoned
savings deposit? The former was a bow of
promise, radiant harbinger of salary checks
to come. The latter was a mere nothing,
parsimoniously doled out to me by a soulless
financial institution, which had not yet
failed. Not even dead and departed dollars
are equal each to each. The dollar or two
you leave behind you in the dining-car is not
equal to the same amount spent on witnessing a play of Bernard Shaw's. When I was a
boy, I found a ten-cent piece under a bench in
a deserted picnic ground. Let no one say that
any other dime in my financial history equals
that one. It was a symbol, not merely of
value, but of romance, of which the find-

ing of lost treasure is one of the classical types.

Dr. John Clifford once remarked that the difference between one man and another is very little, but that little is of very great importance. It is just that most important little that the equation loses sight of. It assumes that one man equals another, which is surely the dullest of human blunders. As soon as we identify our units, the equation's absurdity appears. What is the sum of Mr. Hoover and von Tirpitz? We can only say, Mr. Hoover and von Tirpitz make two literate male human beings. But this is false, for each is more than a literate male human being. What we have been forced to do is to reduce both units to their common terms; and our equation ought, if it is to be true, to read, "Mr. Hoover and von Tirpitz make two literate male human beings, plus all the elements that distinguish each of them from the other."

There are actually people so convinced that one experience is like another that they

have lost that exquisite thing, the capacity
for surprise, and go through life in a state of
virtual insensibility. Some of us, who beguiled our wartime evenings by appearing in
moving-picture theaters disguised as those
prophets of publicity, the Four-Minute Men,
know that no two of these adventures are
alike. Though all managers be polite and au-
diences patient, yet something always marks
the evening with distinction. (I do not, of
course, refer to our speaking.) It would be a
pity to grow callous and lose one's sense for
the variety of these new Arabian Nights.

I went into them, indeed, with my senses
sharpened by a remark of our publicity chairman: "If any of you gets heckled or shot,"
said he, "notify the Publicity Committee."
This personal interest in my fate on the part
of a perfect stranger I found very moving.
About the same time the *London Times* glad-
dened us by reporting, with pardonable ex-
aggeration, that the Four-Minute Men were
each to make ten speeches daily! The powers of the American speech-maker are fully

recognized abroad; he is the automatic among orators.

I shall not soon forget my emotions as I presented myself at my first appointment and sought the manager's face. From the darkness of the spacious interior I caught the music of an organ playing a dirge, and I gained the impression that a funeral was in progress. On entering, I perceived that it was in prospect only, for the action of the drama seemed to be moving inevitably toward one. I sat down close to the screen, upon which a hungry and restless lion alternated with a toothsome child of the softer sex, in tropic garb. I became at once so absorbed in trying to comprehend the situation that I straightway forgot the four heads into which my speech, like the river of Eden, was divided.

A flash uncompromisingly labeled "The End" awoke me to the realization that I, and not the toothsome child, was the victim of the occasion; and with the first letters of "The United States Government Presents"— I was mounting the narrow stair and facing the terrible public. They did not at once attack me, and with a conciliatory sentence I began. Scarce was I embarked upon my first river when a star-shell gracefully ascended from the first balcony, and I knew no more. They had turned the spotlight on me. I forgot my second head and desperately snatched up Hiddekel to replace it, trembling to recall that I had promised them four: four heads in four minutes. What if I had lost Number 2 forever? No, it comes back to me: Gihon! What matters the transposition? War remakes geography; and so on to Euphrates and my closing volley. Even now the lion did not attack, but spared me, rubbing his paws together in satisfaction. Such was my first escape.

I found myself one winter night pushing my way into a theater from which an acolyte was expelling a recreant boy. A crowd of people standing before the doors showed that the house was already full. It had room for six hundred spectators, and they were all there. Five hundred of them seemed to be little boys, and one hundred of these had their caps on. Little boys compose the one element in an audience which will not brook neglect. If they are present, they insist upon your addressing your remarks to them. I had learned this, and acted accordingly. Little boys are not ungrateful, and they are in a position to acknowledge a kindness, for they are masters of the art of applause. These five hundred little boys recompensed me handsomely for my brevity, with a storm of cheers and piercing whistles. How different would have been my fate had I overlooked their highnesses and addressed my remarks to the grown-ups; or had I, like a certain Four-Minute Man I wot of, protracted my discourse to nine minutes! I shudder to think what those little boys would have done to me.

We were talking ships that week, and to my great satisfaction I had two inquirers after the meeting was over. One was a mechanic who wished to enter a shipyard. The other wanted some inside information on whether the following Monday would be heatless, as reported.

Yet ours is a Spartan discipline. The other night I descended from the platform with the warm consciousness of having done my best. In the foyer I met the courteous manager. "I want you to meet Mr. Bumper," said he genially. "Mr. Bumper is one of your men."

Mr. Bumper greeted me without enthusiasm. "You spoke six and a half minutes," said he reproachfully.

The manager came to my relief. "Well, he put it over," said he comfortingly. "No man, I don't care who he is, can tell to a minute how long he's talking. But when they talk for nine minutes, I tell you, I lose money."

I withdrew, crestfallen. They could not realize what an achievement it is for a professor to close in six and a half minutes.

Sometimes we are permitted to speak in theaters of the "legit" type, and as I was about to appear in one of the largest of these,

I asked the obliging doorman about the distribution of his audience. He assured me that they were all over the house, but that the calisthenics were so good that speaking in it was easy. This left me in some doubt as to what might be required of me in the acrobatic line. A picturesque youth, in a caftan and afghan, or some such casual arabesques, conveyed me across the stage to a wicket-gate in the steel curtain, through which I was propelled into the presence of the astonished public for my brief act. You remember Denry making his first speech—how hundreds and hundreds of eyes were fixed piercingly upon him, and after what seemed hours, he heard someone talking. It was himself.

There is a third form of dramatic art to which in the plenitude of my powers I finally attained. It is vaudeville. With some anxiety I looked over the bill in the evening paper, to see what the competition would be, and noted with the greatest interest that it included "Jenks's Mules." Solicitous friends warned me not to get behind these animals;

but when I arrived in the wings, they were stamping and rolling about the stage, and no sooner had the curtain fallen upon their antics than the stage-manager cried sharply, "Come on; this way! You're next!"

I perceived that he was addressing me, so, while he escorted my predecessors downstairs, I set about entertaining his public; and I confess to a certain inward exultation when I saw that the really elegant audience gave me the same polite and absorbed attention they had given to Mr. Jenks's protégés. It is something to know that one can hold the pace even for four minutes with such accomplished quadrupeds. But could I have matched their Elberfeld cousins as successfully in square root?

At our weekly luncheons we exchanged adventures in eloquence and accumulated courage for the week's engagements. One of our most imperturbable comrades was recently speaking in a downtown theater when he noticed that the audience seemed to be looking past him at the curtain behind and

above his head. They next began to point to
it, and finally a friend in the audience cried
out, "Look out, Jim!" He did so, and became aware that the steel curtain had been
silently descending like the bed-canopy in
Conrad's story, and had stopped only a few
inches above his head. It reminded me of a
service on shipboard, when the minister's
white tie broke from its moorings and worked
gradually up toward the top of his collar,
while we were all dreading the moment when
it should pass the summit and dangle about
his neck. The point of resemblance is perhaps slight. It must be the speaker's unconsciousness of a peril which all his hearers saw
but were powerless to avert.

Publicity is, of course, the very breath of
our nostrils, and the other day the talk turned
upon reaching the magazines. A youthful
comrade across the table caught at the suggestion. "If you will get the names of some that
will take our material," said he eagerly, "I
will write the articles myself." I really did
not know how to thank him.

DO ONE AND ONE MAKE TWO?

One of our recent subjects was binoculars, which we asked everybody to turn in for the use of the navy. We also requested the loan of telescopes, spy-glasses, and sextants. In response to these appeals countless binoculars flowed in to the appointed dépôt, and with them a mysterious instrument which our civilian authorities turned over to the chief optician of the city for diagnosis. He unhesitatingly pronounced it a genuine sea-going sextant. So true it is that we do not always recognize the answer to our prayers.

One and one make two! It has a mathematical sound, but we have in this case dragged mathematics whither it would not. It tacitly reduces all men and events to their lowest common terms and, disregarding their differentia, tranquilly proceeds with its meaningless computation. It is the formula of the inexact, the index of

> All the world's coarse thumb
> And finger failed to plumb.

The old vulgar effort to reduce all men to a dead level of uninterest, and all experiences to a dead level of commonplace, finds its justification here. We must not lose the varied flavors of life. Above all, we must not lose discrimination of personality. That would be sacrilege. We have snatched up a mathematical abstraction, true in its limited sphere, and applied it far beyond its proper field, to our own misleading.

The truth is, we must count less. Counting seems a short way to reality. It has its place. But the deeper values of life are not so glibly determined. To this is perhaps due the widespread suspicion of statistics. We distrust these large figures because we know that from every unit covered by them there have been clipped off its distinctive traits, which are not always unessential to the problem. At the bottom of all statistics lies an illusion: that one and one make two.

It is precisely when they are combined that this fundamental unlikeness of units has its most far-reaching consequences. Chemically, one and one may make an explosion. Socially, one and one may make a scene.

DO ONE AND ONE MAKE TWO?

Spiritually, one and one may make a salvation. Who was it that said, "A skin for a skin"? He thought that one man was like another, and that one and one made two.

Hitherto I have reasoned. Let me appeal to authority. The commander of the fortress of Verdun was entertaining some literary visitors. The talk turned upon the Germans. "Ah! the Germans!" said he. "They are not like us. They think that one and one make two."

THE HOUSE OF THE MIND

IT was John Bunyan who long ago wrote
an allegory on the Castle of Mansoul.
Houses are more fashionable than castles
nowadays, and minds, I fear, than souls, and
it is time that someone produced a treatment
of the House of Man's Mind.

It must perhaps be reluctantly admitted
that not every mind merits description under
the figure of a house. For some conventional
intelligences the Flat of the Mind would be
an adequate symbol. Yet at its best estate
the mind is like some spacious mansion with
varied chambers, Victorian or Colonial, but
not without a very comfortable modern wing
for practical convenience. For the mind is
no unalterable house, but a developing structure in which successive historical periods
are reflected, just as they are in the material

fabrics of old seats of learning, in the remodeling of whose very buildings one can read the history of their times.

Only yesterday, the great collegiate houses of the mind were putting on new fronts and adding new wings, to meet the needs of war. Perhaps a tent would be a fitter symbol of these martial additions, for in the autumn of 1918 the universities were military camps. In hundreds of colleges the first academic assembly that year was "At the Flag Pole, at 11:00 A.M., October 1." At that hour, in all these little sisters to West Point, the members of the Student Army Training Corps, one hundred and fifty thousand strong, "pledged their lives to the honor and defense of their country." We felt ourselves in a different world, even from that of last spring. We had given up our favorite courses, our seminars and select groups of graduate students. We were ransacking our past and digging up some less rarefied studies in which we were once, we dimly remembered, counted proficient. The happiest man in this new order was the one who could turn his back upon the specialty of his mature years and teach the military Freshman what the army told us he needed most to learn.

Our colleagues in law and divinity went about disguised as professors of trigonometry and surveying, to which matters, it now appeared, they had devoted their studious youth. Others of us, fearful that such mathematical instruction as we could give might pave the way for military disaster, volunteered for less devious subjects—American history, French, and English composition.

One learned doctor of divinity, on undertaking to renew his youth by imparting trigonometry to the troops, ventured timidly to inquire about the textbook. His mathematical Mentor launched into a glowing account of the work (which it turned out he had written), declaring that it read like a novel and was as simple as a child. My friend hastened to provide himself with this paragon of textbooks. The first sentence that caught his eye was this: "The method pursued in

this book is purely heuristic." This had a re-
assuring sound, but disclosed nothing definite
about the method save that it was clearly
no ordinary one. As the paragon contained
no glossary, and the large dictionary was not
at hand, he took counsel with his erudite
neighbors. Some weakly suggested that it
must be a misprint. Others, under Gallic influence, hazarded that the method was to
study the book only so long as the student
found pleasure in so doing. This interpretation tallied with the conviction general
among instructors that study is now a much
more pleasurable process than it was when
they were students.

The great reading-rooms of the Library
were halls for supervised study for the corps,
each presided over by an officer. For this and
other duties, an initiated friend informed me,
we were to be reinforced with thirty-seven
officers. "Real officers?" I queried doubtful-
ly. "Real officers," he replied a shade stern-
ly. But he was related to Stonewall Jackson
and is not appalled by the atmosphere of war.

THINGS SEEN AND HEARD

It was a stirring sight of an evening to see the companies marching from their several barracks across the moonlit quadrangles to study-hour in those big reading-rooms, with no sound but the regular beat of marching feet and an occasional sharp word of command.

The flag-raising was, indeed, an impressive occasion. Together our academic and military chieftains, across a hollow square flanked by serried masses of civilians, confronted fifteen of the real officers, backed by the Technical Corps in uniform, while a mixed multitude of prospective S.A.T.C. men brought up the rear. "Technical Corps forward—*How!*" shouted the commanding officer. But the Technical Corps for some reason, perhaps for fear of treading on the fifteen real officers, did not advance. "Come right forward, Technical Corps," continued the major soothingly; and the Technical Corps, thus encouraged, advanced with all soldierly propriety a few steps nearer the seat of authority. The bugler blew "To the Colors,'' the flag slowly rose, the officers saluted, the soldiers stood at attention, the civilians took off their hats. Militarization had set in.

The divinity halls were barracks, and so was the football stand. For a time the football team was without a habitation, and the Old Man was desolate. The men's clubhouse was turned over to the Y.M.C.A. The women's clubhouse was a hostess-house, and the deans of women, martially dispossessed of their office rooms, sought temporary shelter in Classics. In a corner of one of the quadrangles is a building modeled on St. John's garden front at Oxford—a gray stone thing of mullioned oriel windows, half hid in clambering ivies. In our upheaval, this mellow and solid fabric became a hut, thus reversing the process applied to ancient Rome by a certain gentleman who found it brick and left it marble.

So was our sanctuary violated, so our fair college turned, not to a hospital, perhaps, but to a military school. It was all reflected in our new vocabulary. The clubhouse had become a hut. The men's halls were barracks. The dining-hall was "mess," not to say "chow." We marched to class (now known, alas, as "school") and recited standing at attention. Mess, drill, school, quarters—in these four life was comprised. The freedom, leisure, and idleness of academic days gave place to the fully prescribed routine of military training. Our sole period of repose was night, which began with taps and ended with what a Freshman described to me as "revelry," thus casting new light upon Byron's famous line,

There was a sound of revelry by night.

Truly we were upheaved. You rose up blithely in the morning, a mere professor of patristics, with not a care in the world and with very few students. You lay down wearily at night, a Y.M.C.A. secretary burdened with the responsibility of a large and crowded hut, with a flourishing canteen, and a staff of three secretaries each more efficient than yourself. And all through no fault of yours;

but solely because the real secretary's passports were unexpectedly ready and he had left for France.

The military transformation was not, indeed, wholly free from minor inconveniences. The first night that guards were set about our Campus Martius a surprising number of suspicious strangers fell into the military net. Library attendants, setting out for home as usual after taps, found their ordinary egress barred by zealous sentries, and were ordered to the other end of the quadrangles. There they encountered an even more resolute sentinel, who improved the opportunity to administer to them an extended reprimand. A zoölogist who had worked late over his experiments was not a little astonished to be halted on the confines of the campus, and narrowly missed exchanging the security of his laboratory for that of the guardhouse. To enter the academic precincts was even more difficult. The janitorial night-shift, coming on for its priestlike task of pure ablution, found the quadrangles like the beleaguered city of Scripture, straitly shut up; none went out and none came in. With such custodians we were surely in no danger of surprise. But it is not a little disconcerting toward the close of a recitation, when the notes of a bugle float in at the open windows, to see your whole class rise as one man and rush from the room, the hindmost, as he disappears, crying over his shoulder, "He's blowing 'Retreat'!"

Not the least benefit of all this upheaval is that it in a measure relieves us from the bondage of books. So short a time ago we cared for nothing but the reading and the writing of books. In this time of war-making the vanity of such pursuits has become clear. A statistical friend informs me that modern publishers turn out almost a hundred thousand different books a year. One shudders to think how many they refuse. The most extraordinary thing about this excessive book-production is that we get on with reading so few of them. The fact is, reading books is not the wholly beneficent exercise it was formerly considered. For one thing, it begets in one a negative and commonplace attitude of mind, and unfits one for free self-expression. I once knew a man who had read so many books that he was quite incapable of independent thought. It is like being led about by the hand until one cannot get around in any other way.

But in the presence of war, actions speak louder than words, and practical studies are to the fore. There was little of the familiar casual attitude until lately fashionable with the modern undergraduate. For all the distractions of orderly duty and supervised study, the Freshman of October, 1918, made a serious business of trying to be both student and soldier. There was a spirit abroad among them which, as one Freshman wrote, "put a new face on the old saying, '*Gott mit Huns*.'" Nothing better illustrates this new spirit than the behavior of the women students. They militarized themselves, and in their Woman Student Training Corps formed an organization with drills, officers, uniforms, a war-service pledge, and a muster-roll almost equal to that of the local S.A.T.C. itself.

Never was academic transformation swifter or more complete, and never did one hold shorter sway. For six weeks to a day this extraordinary experiment linked us to history. It was no small satisfaction to be teaching men, some of whom, as we all believed in October, would soon be officers in the new army. Then came the Armistice. But those morning and evening bugles, and those columns in khaki which made the college a castle, will not soon be forgotten even in the haunts of ancient peace.

If these academic houses have been camps, the individual house of Man's Mind has been in the way of towering again into its old lofty proportions of the Castle of Mansoul, and marks of this period will long be with us in stouter walls and higher turrets. Others not quite so near the scene of conflict have at least forsaken the rich and quiet chambers of the mind to build and occupy new quarters suited to the hour.

THE HOUSE OF THE MIND

He can have given little thought to his own mind who does not see in it a complex structure, with many rooms that are far from modern. Everybody, one observes, is orthodox in some phase of his thinking; that is, there are some old rooms in his mind which he has not yet remodeled. Nor are these older chambers of the mind tenantless. In many a one of them dwells the spirit of some ancestor who added it to our mental establishment. For the mind is in a measure an inheritance, however much we may be responsible for the furniture we put into it. It is partly the society of these old fellows that makes these chambers of the mind attractive or otherwise. Who has not felt, in moments of sheer enjoyment, the disapproving presence of some stiff old Puritan forefather to whom all pleasure was anathema, and has not forthwith fled to some sunnier mental spaces where he could not follow? For these subtenants of ours, as if bedridden, cannot leave the quarters they have bequeathed to us. It would not be possible to

[73]

get them all down to the dining-room together, to devour, say, a good book with
you. And if it could be done, probably no
single book would hold the interest of all
these diversities.

What with construction and addition,
some minds come to be of palatial proportions, richly furnished by reading, travel,
and observation, looking out through many
windows upon fair prospects and far horizons. They are affluent, tranquil, settled
abodes, in which the occupant lives busily,
yet at ease. Their cupboards and storerooms
quickly yield what you are in search of, in
the way of fact, opinion, or reaction. It is
not alone that they contain much, but their
contents seem to be so conveniently and
accessibly disposed. These are the palatial
minds, the houses of the mental aristocracy.
They have many chambers, some looking
westward over the fruitful past, but others
to the east and the expectant future. For
these houses are not mere treasuries of old
values. Their occupants will show you many

a new acquisition, with all the zest of the discoverer. Only these have not destroyed the proportion and perspective of the possessor, or made him forgetful of his other goods of longer standing. In minds like these you can wander for hours, finding new treasures, interests, and outlooks. We stay in them with a sense of luxury, and we leave them with a feeling of deprivation.

One sometimes finds his way into minds less spacious and well-ordered. Some are small but exquisitely furnished, and with their one or two rooms make delightful visiting. They have a genial atmosphere that is lacking in many a grander house.

Whatever be the origin or extent of the mental habitations that we occupy, for their furniture we are responsible. A common scheme of mental furnishing consists of a few prejudices inconspicuously placed where the chance visitor will stumble over them. Once, as I was playing the fourth hole of a western golf course, a man driving by in a wagon stopped to offer me a golf-ball that he had found, and pressed it upon me as a free gift until I could not very well refuse. He then invited me to enter his mind, which I did. It was not large, but it was a busy place, elaborately furnished with prejudices of the most substantial sort. He expounded to me the war, which, it developed, was nothing less than the irrepressible conflict between Romanism and Free-Masonry. The war has led to a remarkable airing out of the cupboards of the mind, and some very quaint furniture has incidentally been exposed to neighborly observation.

Not only in the amount and arrangement of their furniture, but in its character, minds differ very much. Some admit nothing but the latest thing, and think shame to show anything as old as last season. Others exhibit only second-hand articles. In the bric-à-brac of such a mind you encounter a host of jokes and anecdotes which bring back your lost youth. One sometimes meets men whose minds are furnished exclusively in the style of the eighteenth century—and unfortunate-

ly not always with the genuine antiques.
And what a treatise might be written upon
mental housekeeping: how windows should
be kept clean, the furniture frequently shift-
ed and overhauled, and grievances aired as
little as possible and only when nobody is
about.

The most gracious aspect of a house is its
hospitality. Some guests we admit to certain
chambers but never think of entertaining in
others. They would not understand or enjoy
them. So it comes about that the same mind
shows very different sides to different visitors. One you admit at once to the living-
room; another never gets farther than the re-
ception-room. A third has but to show himself to be ushered into the intimacy of the
garden or the study; and a fourth may come
in without ringing, and you will cheerfully
take him with you over the whole house
from attic to cellar. For friendship is to have
the latchkey of another's mind.

It is clearly the business of the mind to
build it more stately mansions as the swift

seasons roll. For the mind cannot remain fixed, no matter what the Psalmist thought about the heart. Ourselves, like everything and everybody else, must change. Here we have been misled by what we may call the delusive fixity of art. Art has beguiled us and we have been beguiled. In all its forms it has conspired to create in us the conviction that life, when it has attained a certain estate, becomes stationary. Everything about art is calculated to give one that settled impression. It has taught us to expect fixity, whereas life shows us only endless process and function, to which in mind and body we must conform.

Our minds are filled with these images of art, and upon them we unconsciously frame our thinking. But they are not real. Even the realities for which they stand are constantly changing. Your friends and associates of last year are now lieutenants, captains, majors, colonels. They are not the same. The very nations are not the same. What were Ukrainia and Czechoslovakia when you last went abroad? Can the mind then remain the same? It is a painful business living in a house that is being remodeled, and doubly so when it is the house of the mind. But in a world of new forces and changed faces, when a new thoroughfare is being opened through the mental property of each of us, it is not enough to withdraw into our mental habitations and shut the door. We must change our minds.

THE SPIRITS OF OUR SIRES

SOME literary persons, poets and the like, profess to find great inspiration in the spirit of their sires. Just as they are fainting under the burdens of life, that mysterious influence comes to their relief, and rouses their better selves. They seem to have no difficulty in recognizing the spirit, and gather from it just what they want. It is all very simple and practical.

My own experience is very different. Not that I am unconscious of the persistent influence of my sires. On the contrary, my difficulty is in escaping from them. They seem determined to direct my activities as well as their own. Worst of all, there is no unanimity among them as to what I am to do in this or that situation. Indeed, my relation to my affairs is often reduced to that of the chairman of a somewhat turbulent committee, each member of which is trying to impose his will upon the rest. If he succeeds, I have the disagreeable duty not only of carrying out his wishes, but of trying to reconcile the disaffected majority to the course adopted. It is this mutual disagreement among my sires that I find so harassing.

They are to begin with of the most diverse types and tastes. I learned the other day that a Dutchman dislikes to do anything in a hurry, and I instantly recognized a leading trait of the Center of my personal Reichstag. This consists of a group of quiet but determined characters very well satisfied with the world as it is, very reluctant about taking any new steps, and very slow in taking any steps at all. With this extreme conservatism about exertion of any sort, these worthies combine a fanatically obstinate adhesion to any course they may have entered upon, even when it has shown itself to be unwise and impossible. They do not know how to let go. If they have once begun a thing, they will hang on to the bitter end, no matter how clear the folly of such persistence may become even to themselves. These persons are thoroughly Dutch in their aversion for doing things in haste. They prefer to look a piece of work all over before they attempt it. Circumspection, not to say suspicion, is their way. There is nothing of the experimentalist about them. They cannot work in a hurry. If they are forced to do so, they usually steal back to the job afterward and do it over.

The sire who not infrequently compels these reputable Dutchmen to this humiliating course is the *enfant terrible* of the whole company. I have often wished I could identify him more definitely, but as I have known so few of these gentlemen personally, I can only conjecture that he was an Irishman who flourished in the state of New York about a century ago. It is he who throws the Dutch contingent into utter confusion by rising very early in the morning (a thing they detest), and buoyantly beginning some visionary but laborious undertaking which they have afterward, thanks to their temperamental obstinacy, to carry to completion. This Irish member is, in fact, as hasty and precipitate as his compeers are cautious and slow, and the most painful ructions necessarily ensue. He is pliant, sanguine, and credulous. He exercises an influence upon the common counsels out of all proportion to his numbers. When his persuasive loquacity prevails over the sounder sense of the Low Countries faction, I find myself consenting to give lectures, write articles, and even lend money. For these excesses the Dutch afterward castigate me cruelly, while my Irish friend as often as not absents himself altogether from the labors into which he has betrayed me.

I think it must be this same Irish chap who is so negligent about putting away my books, tools, and clothes. He once, coming home in a bad frame of mind, mislaid a valuable article of mine, which has never been recovered. The Dutch group generously waived their traditional grievance and joined loyally in the search; in fact, they are still searching, but the Irishman and I know that it will never be found, and he sometimes gets quite gloomy over it, for he is of course a moody and mercurial individual.

This untidiness of my Irish relative is in some measure offset by the efforts of those indomitable Hollanders who have a positive mania for picking up and putting things to rights. They go around after him and do all that man can do to gather up his scattered effects and fold and put away his clothes. If he carelessly throws an empty envelope away in the street, they will oblige me to turn back and pick it up. Once in a while, of course, something escapes them. He comes in late and leaves his trousers in a heap on the radiator, to their unspeakable disgust when they find them there next morning.

Yet the Irishman is a good-natured, well-meaning chap, and my friends decidedly prefer him to his Dutch confrères. He is a sociable, talkative being, and I try to take him along when I am confronted with a dinner or some less formidable social engagement. He is generally glad to get away from the Dutchmen, whose meticulous methods distress him sorely; and if I can keep him from taking offense at some fancied slight or other during the soup or fish course (he is fearfully sensitive), and can restrain his loquacity after the roast appears, things go fairly well. Anyway it is better than taking the Dutchmen out in company, for they care nothing about it and seldom do anything but frown stupidly upon the scene. The Irishman, however, is profoundly romantic and sentimental, and loves to relate commonplace experiences of mine as if they were his own. He is, in fact, decidedly facetious, but if anyone ventures to say so, he is fearfully dashed, and lapses into a moody silence.

Between the deadly uniformity of the Dutchmen's behavior and the complete lack of it in the Irishman's, I am sometimes wearied out, and I take refuge from the strife of tongues in the society of a very different ancestor of mine. He is an Englishman, and

[85]

I am very much afraid he would qualify as a Junker. But he is an easy-going, phlegmatic individual, and he never makes me uncomfortable. In fact, he seems to know how to make both himself and me very comfortable, indeed. He is a past master at taking his ease; there is nothing he likes so much to take. He never bothers much with the contentions of the others; but if either of them accomplishes anything he is as pleased over it as though he had done it himself. In fact, he seems to think he has. He rarely goes out into society; he prefers to have his friends come to see him, and sends the Irishman to return their visits. When he entertains, which is about the only activity he indulges in, he prefers to have the lesser breeds kept in the background, leaving him to do the honors. He has no accomplishments of any sort, except that he is a good listener, and likes to start his guests on what he wants to hear and they want to say. He has a sort of stolid family pride, as though he were descended from the Plantagenets, though there is no evidence at all for any such descent. His highest faculty is that of savoring the good of life. He does not frantically pursue it; he simply knows it when he gets it, and knows how to appreciate it. I hope to spend my time increasingly in his society as I grow old.

It may be that some people manage the spirits of their sires less democratically than I do mine; that they domineer over them. At least, I am well aware that most people seem to have no difficulty with them. Perhaps they give little attention to the voices of these worthies, and are satisfied to rule their spirits with an autocratic hand. But anyone who is conscious of the diverse personal strains within him must sometimes feel that he is the seat of a sort of senior republic, over which he is called to preside, and the mandates of which he is bound to perform. And so we become each of us, at his best estate, a little parable of democracy.

I cannot boast a multiple personality, nor have I ever been of pathological interest to psychologists, yet I sometimes wonder if I am any more than just one of my forefathers after another. They are like the Officer of the Day, successively captain of my soul. We know, of course, very little about most of those through whom the gift of life has come down to us. But when we look back upon those of them we have known and through our aunts and uncles dimly see the forms of others, we see enough often to recognize in their behavior somewhat characteristic reactions of our own. I wonder whether if we could really know our forebears for two hundred years back even, we would not find in that goodly company of perhaps two hundred and fifty people most of our most valued personal traits. One or another of them, I feel sure, would exhibit the same indolence or energy, the same physical inertia and mental activity, or physical energy and mental reluctance, the same readiness or procrastination, the same love of hardship or of ease, the same instinctive propensity to get under the world's burdens or to let the other fellow walk the floor, the same restless passion for travel or the same dread of removal as of its greatest example, death. The plain truth is we are shockingly like our sires, and not always only the best of them either, and telephones and automobiles have altered their fundamental traits far less than we fondly think.

Of course, the sheer numerousness of one's progenitors if one reckons far enough back reduces this to the mere commonplace of human nature. I am a poor statistician, but has not someone remarked that everybody living today is related, distantly, of course, to almost everybody that was living when Troy fell or Rome was founded? But my race memories are not, like Mr. Jack London's, of a remote and atavistic sort. He could recall swinging from limb to limb with the tree-people. I am speaking of our more proximate ancestors from whom we may suppose that we more characteristically derive. And my contention is that these worthies live again in our behavior, and while we go about as we suppose thinking our own thoughts and minding our own affairs, we are really most of the time repeating their sacrifices or indulgences, their ambitions or caprices. This must be why we so often, in fancy, glance down long avenues of existence we know we shall never enter ourselves. To this unassimilated complexity of ancestors is due, in part, that interior maladjustment which is the great drawback about being a child. It is partly that we in our untrained youth can conceive a great many things quite beyond our powers of execution; but mainly that our ancestors from Adam to Paterfamilias are still at war in our members, in a sort of spiritual Armageddon. It is chaos and revolution, until the warring factions come to an equilibrium.

The more I reflect upon my progenitors and their respective contributions to what I consider my temperament, the more fervently I wish I might have known them more widely and well. Not that I would blame them, still less praise them. But it might help me to understand myself a little better. I know a man of so ancient a family that his principal ancestors for quite four hundred years are well known to him. Such familiarity must make it easy to catalogue every passing trait of the rising generation, not to say of one's own wayward spirit. "How strange Gwendolen is today!" "Well, they say the maternal grandmother of the fourth marchioness was always like that." This sort of thing certainly has its dangers. Someone has explained the genius of Mr. Winston Churchill (Britannicus) for military strategy by his descent from the Prince of Commanders who went to the War in Flanders. I have even been told that the second Duke of Wellington believed military genius to be his birthright, although he betrayed no signs of such an endowment.

But most of us know most of our lineage chiefly through their inward survivals in our degenerate selves. Perhaps we are freer so, and not less happy. I have read of an ancient relative of mine who in 1665 offended another loyal subject of the crown, by "charging him to be a lyer, and that he had stolen his kidd," and he was called upon by a Colonial justice to pay twenty pounds damages or apologize. Now Roger, I doubt not, was a man of spirit, but he apologized. Is not he that ruleth his spirit greater than he that taketh a city?

Why not capitalize our ancestors? Their capability must in essence be at our disposal. We "have it in us," as we say. Here is our equipment for the exigencies of life. If the day is fair and not a sail in sight, pipe all hands on deck to paint and polish, or aloft to mend the rigging. If a pirate appears on the weather bow, clear the decks for action and call stout Uncle Anthony, who fell in the Indian mutiny, to the quarter-deck. Is Cleopatra's barge coming down the river? Get the lubbers below and have the Irishman up to show the gentleman he is. Yes, individually they have their uses. And in proportion as we consciously or not get our spiritual household disciplined and responsive, so

that each will instinctively present himself
when he is needed, we accomplish our own
individuality. It lies in the variations possible for each of us. We differ not so much in
character as in our peculiar combinations of
characters, and in the ones we let predomi-
nantly control us. This is why some people
are so kaleidoscopic. The adepts say the
mind is like a cake of ice—or shall we more
nobly say an iceberg?—mostly submerged in
unconsciousness. The more dense of us naturally sink lower, floating as it were all but
awash in the unconscious. Obviously it matters much which of our characters we wear
uppermost, and sometimes it becomes very
desirable that the iceberg should topple
completely over and expose a fresh surface
to the air. Versatility consists in changing
guard now and then and occasionally letting
our Celtic, Gallic, and Teutonic ancestors
out to have their say—within reason.

It is not as individuals, however, but
collectively that I most prize this garrison
of ancestral spirits holding the fortress of

Mansoul. If you attend a hearing at the City Hall and the assistant corporation counsel rebukes you, and the billboard attorneys berate you as a busybody because your municipal interest extends beyond your own doorstep, and underlings bellow at you as though you were deaf, and hirelings of monopoly shoot out the lip at you and gnash upon you with their teeth, you wither a little under the universal disapprobation. You feel strangely alone. Such is the lot of the mere private citizen in the stronghold of his representatives. You never realized before how private a citizen you were. Now at length you know yourself for a single individual and hardly that. But just as you feel your back is to the wall, reinforcements arrive. Knowledge of your danger has reached the spirits of your sires and up from below they come swarming to your relief. An individual only? You are much more than that. You are a whole tribe. The life of ancient nations is gathered up in you, and this collective consciousness carries annoyance and isolation down before it by sheer weight of numbers. The forces that threatened your spirit dwindle to their normal proportions, and their blustering voices sink to a plaintive buzz. Your ancestors have delivered you, not by their renown, but simply by their multiplicity of attitudes and points of view, which puts your momentary panic into its true perspective.

But no reflections upon this subject would be complete which did not include the matter of spiritual disinheritance. We all know those figures in fiction who harshly cut off offending heirs with a shilling. What shall be thought of those forebears of mine who were financiers and money-makers who refuse to participate in the activities of my personal Duma and systematically absent themselves from its proceedings? If one of them would but condescend to take his turn at the supervision of my affairs! I would guarantee that no wastrel ne'er-do-weel of the shadowy company should squander the proceeds of his efforts. I remember hearing of one of them who at some troubled epoch lost ten thousand pounds in the fall of stocks in a single day. But what a man to have had all those pounds! He must have gotten them somehow. They do not seem so colossal today, but in the days of the Four Georges—! It must have been Napoleon's activities that beared the market, which reminds me that it was Wilhelm II whose going forth to war broke my bank. There is encouragement in this. Evidently I am in my modest measure in the same financial succession with my ancestor, at least as far as war losses are concerned. Or was it in 1793 when the death of Louis XVI sent consols tumbling that my poor grandsire lost his myriad Louis? At any rate, it is not just to transmit to helpless posterity the credulity which loses money without the Midas touch which conjures it together.

But perhaps he did in the days of my inconsiderate childhood lift up his thrifty voice in the wilderness of my soul and find no response, and so subside so far as I was con-

cerned forever. Maybe the fault was mine.
Certainly others of our own blood have fallen heir to qualities we brothers and sisters
of theirs are strangers to. We look with wonder at their affinity for responsibility or action. They are out in the ways of men while
we in a chimney corner sit dreaming over a
book. What has been left out of our makeup?
An ancestor, of course. There is an ancestor missing. Either he has fallen overboard
through our neglect, or he was loitering
ashore and never shipped with us at all.

Have I seemed to speak lightly of our progenitors? But would it become me to detail
their finer qualities which I detect at work
within my complex ego? Yet one saying of
one of them I must approve, and carry with
me to my dying day, when I propose more
than ever to recall it. He was an old man,
dying among the New England hills where
he had spent his life, and as he looked forth
at them under the summer sun, he said wist-
fully, "It is a beautiful world to leave."I do
not think Homer could have said it better.

THE NEW BARBARISM

THE deviser of the electric bell has probably long since gone where all janglings cease, but his alarming contrivance is with us still. The evil that men do lives after them, as even Mark Antony observed; and sometimes the ingenuity of it blinds us to its darker side. How happy any gong-banging savage would have been, had he been able to rig up an arrangement to keep his gong banging continually while he sat back and reveled in the noise! But would he have been any less a savage for his success?

Once, and once only, have I encountered barbarism—that is, if one may say so, barbarism proper. I left by the first boat, but before it called, I had registered three definite impressions. They were Noise, Odor, and Confusion. Of course, there were other minor ones. There was no water even to wash with; and one felt a general insecurity of life and liberty, a certain well-known English resident having been freshly kidnapped and held for ransom. But these were incidents. The others were fundamental.

As we dropped anchor off the mole, a crowd of barbarians made their appearance on shore, yelling and gesticulating in the wild, cannibalistic manner well known to readers of Tartarin and Crusoe. If it had not been for the providential appearance of a representative of Mr. Cook, we might have thought twice about landing. The yelling, which had come faintly to us on the ship's deck, became pandemonium when we arrived upon the mole. There seemed to be no method in it, each man merely shouting his loudest in sheer excitement. It was the voice of barbarism upraised in salute to civilization.

But at five o'clock of a dark winter afternoon, when stores and offices are closing, and streets are packed with hurrying throngs, you stand on the pavement waiting to cross the crowded street, amid the warning notes of motors, the shrill whistles of policemen, and the rush of clanging trolley-cars, the whole fitfully illumined by an arc light, and the elevated roaring deafeningly overhead— and you ask, Is this civilization? Does the mere fact that all this din and confusion are mechanically produced really make them civilized? Or is it only the big brother of barbarism?

The old barbarism exulted in Noise, Sensation, and Slaughter. But how poor were its achievements in these directions beside those of the new. And what, in the name of fair play, could their poor old lungs and tom-toms accomplish against those modern marvels, the whistle, the siren, and the cut-out? At a recent dinner of patriotic speakers, the occasion was enlivened by a Jackies' band. Upon the illimitable spaces of the high seas, its appalling clamor might have melted into music; but in a small dining-room, seating only a thousand or so, the finer effects were lost. I was surrounded by great conversers, but against that avalanche of sound they were as impotent as I. We read one another's lips a while, then simply clung to our chairs and waited, till

> Silence like a poultice came
> To heal the blows of sound.

And odors! Those of barbarism are strong for a mile or two, but they cannot carry like those of civilization. All the scents of Araby and Cologne could not disguise the odor that one beneficent industry daily distills upon one million of my fellow-citizens. My own experience of it runs back only some fifty years; but it is not new. Only it grows stronger and more analyzable as the years roll by. The poet's leagues of odor puts it none too strong.

On summer evenings the train often bears me along a beautiful stream, winding between wooded banks, and breaking now and again into waterfalls and rapids. Beyond it, the sinking sun gilds the fleecy clouds, and all their sunset glories are mirrored in the brimming river. The soft air of evening floats in at the windows, fragrant with forest odors. Everything conspires to soothe the jaded senses, until we reach the vicinity of the paper mill, when the fragrance is suddenly displaced by something quite different, but fully equal to anything I can recall in my brief visit to barbarism.

Barbarism rejoices greatly in display, in feathers, beads, and warpaint—which brings us to the delicate and difficult subject of dress and jewels. As respects woman's use of these let us content ourselves with remarking that there are few jewels that seem really to enhance beauty. But when one sees his fellow-men wearing diamond studs in negligee shirts already equipped with their full complement of buttons, one is really at a loss to determine whether this be the new barbarism or the old.

And when the weather is raw and unfavorable, and the golfers few upon the links, and I hear a shrill chorus of chattering voices from the caddie-house; or when the skating-house is full of uproarious boyhood shouting meaninglessly together, I know it for the voice of the old barbarism lifted by our youth in the savage stage of development, through which, according to a well-known theory of social evolution, we all must pass—if so be we do indeed pass through it and emerge safely on the farther side.

Barbarism, no doubt, saw more of slaughter than do we; but the old yearning for it will not die, and we certainly make the most of what we have. We film it, headline it, and chart it, until it becomes a staple feature of our daily life. Like Dryden's Alexander, thrice we slay the slain, and the most Cowperian of us would feel a haunting void were it withdrawn. There is still a strain in us that calls for a certain amount of bloodshed, real or imaginary, to be enjoyed, if not experienced. Mere accidents, it is to be observed, do not satisfy this craving.

How our sensibilities are harrowed by the inexplicable disappearance of a little girl from some household previously unknown to fame! What has become of her? Has she been eaten by a bear, or fallen into the lake, or run away with the butcher? All these promising clues are followed out in turn by the faithful, relentless, and sleuthlike press, but alike in vain. If our interest does not wane, we are gratified (or disappointed) to learn that, in sober fact, she had gone on a visit to her aunt in the country, and had not been seeing the papers there. Fatal omission! One cannot safely refrain from seeing the papers, if only to keep them from getting the idea that one is missing, and investing one with an air of sinister and tremendous mystery before one knows it. For, after such investiture, it is useless to explain, protest, or deny. One remains a being of mystery, a person with a past, obstinately carrying one's hollow secret with one to the grave.

Nor is the new barbarism without its religion. In all great cities it rears its spacious temples, with vast naves rich with bronze and marble. Upon a kind of pulpit high above the throng appears at intervals the muezzin of the cult, and intones his litany: "The train—is now ready—for De Kalb—Marshalltown — Omaha — Cheyenne — Salt Lake City —San Francisco—and Los Angeles —The Pacific Limited — leaving — at ten-thirty—from Track 3." This is no inconsiderable art; for he pauses after each measure, until the last great, true note dies away; and he keeps his voice to the last syllable on the same level tone. Not even on "Track 3" does it descend. The effect is stately, liturgical, worthy of its splendid setting. And the worshipers seated in the pews at once rise up in obedience to his call, and move silently out to Track 3. Even we who are left behind know something of their exalted mood, for has not the muezzin with his chant sent our thoughts hurrying over the plains and Rockies to the coast, and conjured up within us many a rich memory and high aspiration?

If transcontinental departures are events, still more are such arrivals. You stand at the gate with a throng of expectant sons, mothers, and daughters, and the California train pulls slowly and interminably in. From it emerge in a triumphal procession the hadjis, the devotees of travel, a fanatical gleam in their eyes, the bright light of achievement upon their faces. They have arrived!

No religion is worth anything without hardship, and the new one has its share. You will spend hot hours of a July evening, waiting in line by the hotter kitchen of the dining-car for a chance to sit down and be fed. Or you will dash off at so-called eating-stations, and snatch a hasty meal, or purchase a sodden cake right out of the refrigerator. You will toss restlessly in chilly uppers or gasp in stifling lowers. You will sit for hours on observation platforms, long after observation has ceased to be a pleasure. You will see the frost gather on every bit of metal in your car, and the desert sands will sift in about you unto suffocation. But you will travel. Nothing can stop you. As for these light afflictions, you will glory in them. Such is religion.

THE NEW BARBARISM

And who does not know the sects and schisms of travel?—how some swear by Florida, and some by California, while others find salvation only in Canada, Alaska, or the Orient; but each is forever dinning in your ears the dogmas of his cult.

Nor is the new religion without its adepts. I met one of them once—a child not yet in her teens, yet set apart as a devotee of travel. Her sole interest was to inquire how many times one had crossed the ocean. If but six times, one was naught; she had crossed twelve—or was it sixteen? With her, at any rate, it was something more than an annual experience. But that was years ago. Nowadays the question is, how many times have you been round the world? A colonel told me the other day that he had been round twice in one year. I wish he and the little girl, now grown no doubt to fanatical womanhood, might meet.

Of course, travel has its high days, its pilgrimages, its evangelistic literature, designed to implant in the minds of the stay-at-home public, if such there be, an insatiable yearning for it. It has even its daily exercises. I, unfortunately, can walk in three minutes from the garden gate to the museum where I muse for a living. But I have, therefore, no opportunity to progress in the new cult such as is enjoyed by my neighbors, who travel from eight to twenty-eight miles to business every morning. Still more blest are those whose duties call them every week or two to New York or Washington.

A rich store of common experience binds these travel-adepts together. Once, on the ocean, I sat at table with a certain much-traveled man, of large and placid habit, whose wont it was, at dinner, after the steward had conferred upon each of us our ration of six raw oysters, to beckon the man to his side and devour any surplus. He could inform us just how many of them one was likely to get with one order at each of the leading American hotels. I, in my superficiality, had never realized that such inequalities existed.

THE NEW BARBARISM

In the mountains of Kentucky, we are told, if a girl marries and settles twenty miles from home, her family definitely resigns all expectation of seeing her again this side of heaven. But we less sheltered beings think nothing of journeying that far for dinner, or even tea. To be deterred by an insubstantial consideration like distance would argue a fatal weakness of the modern mind. It would violate the new religion, the purpose of which is the annihilation of distance.

An aerial friend assures me that he has taken breakfast and dinner in Fresno, and lunched the same day in Coronado, over three hundred miles away. In one of the chief seats of the new barbarism a favorite afternoon diversion is motoring past forty miles of billboards, embodying the very purest traditions of savage art; a sight to gladden the paleolithic decorator of the cavern of Altamira. And the other day, in the seclusion of a western golf-club, one man was telling another how Tom Jones had motored down from San Francisco to Los Angeles in twenty-three hours; to which the other irreligiously replied, "What delayed him?"

But it is in its ways of trade that barbarism is most instructive. The street vendor cries his wares through the city, and will pursue you far with his insistent demands that you buy. The shop-keeper will follow for blocks, with his patter of rapidly falling prices. In rural Egypt, in former days, if you wished to hire a donkey, you had first to hire a man to protect you from the rabble of donkey-boys from which you were to choose. With resounding blows of his staff, he would keep them from actually riding you down in their determination to win your trade. The insistence of trade and the violence of competition are stable features of barbarism.

We do these things a little more subtly, perhaps—or, should we say, more crudely? In effect, if not in person, the peddler hounds us through the town, by day and night. If we ascend into the street cars, he is there. If we motor over the boulevards, he is there. If we open a magazine or a program, he is there.

THE NEW BARBARISM

If we look over our morning mail, he is there. If the telephone rings, he is there, desiring to take our photograph or clean our rugs and curtains. His hand is under the door with a dodger, and up the telegraph pole with a placard. Night itself does not obscure him.

The old barbarism was undoubtedly gossipy and scandalous. But it did not gossip and scandalize in editions of half-a-million copies. The old barbarism was hideous, vulgar, and noisome. But it did not have all the resources of machinery and capital to help keep it so. The old barbarism was noisy and dirty; but the distribution of dirt in barbarism is nowhere nearly as efficient and constant as in civilization. As a great prima donna remarked the other morning, "I have washed my hands fifteen times today already, but I love your city." The whole population of the metropolis where I reside is each day evenly and patiently coated with soot, and will certainly end by going over to the pigmented races which we have so long misprized.

THINGS SEEN AND HEARD

I once had occasion to walk across the Nile Valley at Abydos, a distance of some eight miles, to catch the Cairo train. As it was market-day, the little winding path across the cultivation was dotted with groups of peasants, old and young, journeying in my direction; and many a courteous old Egyptian, seeing me hurrying along, alighted from his camel or donkey to offer me a ride. Perhaps it was their gentle influence that led me the other evening, as I was returning from the City of Destruction in a crowded railway train, to yield to a chivalrous impulse and, at the risk of having to stand up for twelve minutes, offer a young woman my seat. Before she could take it, an old gentleman, surely devoid of all nobler qualities, slipped nimbly into it, leaving the baffled young woman to languish in the perpendicular, until the neighboring sitters adroitly crowded together enough to make a fractional place for her, in which she continued her journey.

But then, of course, Egypt is one of the most ancient seats of civilization.

DEMOCRACY DELVED INTO

IT is said that in ancient times there lived in Libya a man named Apsethus, who cherished the laudable ambition of being considered a god. Being a resourceful person and perceiving that the Libyans like other peoples were a credulous folk, he collected a large number of parrots and taught them to say "Apsethus is a god." When the parrots had thoroughly mastered this lesson, he set them at liberty, and they dutifully flew all over Libya, crying, "Apsethus is a god." This indisputable testimony of nature speedily converted the Libyans to his cult, and he found himself the recipient of divine honors.

This easy scaling of Olympus came to the attention of one of those marplots of antiquity, the Greeks, and he put himself upon the case as a special detective. Whether he cross-examined one of the parrots I do not know, but he somehow learned enough to take a leaf from the book of the new divinity. He collected a still larger number of parrots and taught them to say, "Apsethus caged us and forced us to say he was a god." When the parrots were letter perfect in this new lesson the ingenious Greek sent them forth to undermine the faith of the simple Libyans. Whereupon, says the historian, the Libyans having heard the recantation of the parrots, came together and unanimously decided to burn Apsethus.

The story of Apsethus often recurs to my mind as I pick up the morning paper and hear the voices of the parrots crying that this one or that one is or is not a god. Who has not in these latter days encountered full many a gullible old fowl which reversed itself with all the swiftness and completeness of Apsethus' missionaries? And of course no one blames it any more than the Libyans blamed the parrots. But no doubt the story has other applications hardly less edifying. The world

is fairly full of people who go about simply
repeating what they have heard or read.
How many of us, indeed, do anything else,
when an expression of opinion—social, political, or religious—is in order?

It is at least evident that there was something very fine and democratic about Libyan
religion and theology as illustrated in the
cult of Apsethus. Of course, they did too
easily accept the testimony of the parrots,
but in this they are unfortunately not alone.
Indeed, it is precisely here that their experience is modern and representative. The Libyans did not stop to inquire how the parrots
came by their information. It was enough
that they were parrots. The strength of Apsethus' method lay in this, that he appealed
to democracy. *Vox Papagai, Vox Populi.* His
error, if he made any, was in forgetting that
everybody's believing something does not of
itself make it true. Even democracy would
not bear the strain he put upon it.

It is interesting to look abroad and observe what diverse things are predicated of

democracy. A distinguished gentleman recently declared that a marked characteristic
of the late German army was its democracy.
In support of this thesis he cited an incident
observed and greatly enjoyed by the recent
ruler of Germany who, while motoring as
usual between fronts, overtook a soldier
driving a herd of swine. The Kaiser asked
the soldier what his occupation was in time
of peace, and the soldier replied that he was
a professor in the University of Göttingen.
This was hailed by the Kaiser and his pub-
licist as a convincing proof of the thoroughly democratic character of the German army:
the professor a swineherd.

This incident and the interpretation there-
of suggest a flood of reflections. Does democracy indeed mean that every man shall be set
to doing something to which he is unaccustomed and for which he is unfitted? This
view is unfortunately not confined to the
Kaiser and his interpreter. To the same
school belongs that definition of autocracy
put forward in 1917 by a kindred spirit. This

much-talked-of autocracy, said he, is really nothing more nor less than administration by experts.

There is, of course, nothing more common than claiming everything in sight for your favorite institution. A very able man of science once informed me that the whole hope of human betterment lay with the universities. Another declared, in my hearing, that wars and international misunderstandings would never be done with until the science of geography came into its rightful place in human thought. I have heard a prominent representative of trades unionism assert that we owe our free schools, free speech, and free press to the trades unions. I confess I had been accustomed to ascribe these beneficent institutions to other sources, and I was shocked to reflect that if he was so mistaken I might be also.

In this horrible reflection lies, I believe, the kernel of democracy. The other party wins the national election. We all know the awful sense of impending disaster that attends the defeat of our side at the polls. Shall we at once put an end to this miserable existence then, or shall we linger on to succumb to the inevitable cataclysm? But stay! Democracy whispers, There remains always this possibility, faint indeed and infinitely remote, yet still a possibility: The other man may be right, after all.

Elections! Ah, the elections! If war was the sport of kings elections are the sport of democracy. What races at Epsom, Longchamps, or Latonia attract such attention as a presidential election? Think of the night of election day! And think how on far-off Asiatic steppes strange men clad in sheepskin who never heard of Maude S. or the America's Cup will inform one another that the great Lord Wilson has beaten the great Lord Hughes and been elected president (as they fondly think) of America.

After elections, democracy has no more characteristic feature than the finance campaign. We are told that Turkey, immediately upon being as she supposed liberated by the young Turks and transformed into a democracy, entered upon a finance campaign to secure by popular subscription a fund to buy two warships from the British government. And what with our Liberty Loans and the Victory Loan and Red Cross drives and all the unofficial ones that have followed in their wake no one in the United States can have escaped this mighty engine of democracy. Telephone, telegraph, and mail system run its errands, newspapers and billboards do its bidding. Society, business and religion, the church, the lodge and the grange, unite to further it. It has its union button, which marks its ransomed subscriber off from the outcast residue of mankind, but must be replaced next week with the newer button of the next campaign. It sets us studying one another's financial, social, and philanthropic status as never before. We become suddenly interested to know the whereabouts of this man and that. Is he in town? Or is he in Florida or California? When will he return? Heaven send it be not too late.

But if it be, let him be wired, and wired again. Who knows him? Who knows him best? Who knows him unrefusably well? How shall he be approached? What are his habits? Does he like to lead, or prefer to follow? Shall we strike high or low? Is he gregarious, or does he play a lone hand? Truly in a democracy, the proper study of mankind is man.

There is something childlike, too, about democracy. It rejoices in being robbed, and advertises the fact upon the housetops until one wonders why any reasonably observant person should not avail himself of this short and easy way to private affluence and public admiration. No princely act of beneficence, no achievement of sagacity or courage, could possibly win more swift and admiring attention than the theft of a few thousand dollars regularly evokes from the headline artist and the paragrapher. That crime is mostly a manifestation of weakness does not enter the mind of the journalistic interpreter of democracy. To him, and we must suppose to the generality of his readers, crime is a cause for thrilling wonder, and nothing more.

A young physician whose friends were sympathizing with him on the hardships of night work in his profession reassured them by saying that the day of that sort of thing was really past; people weren't sick at night much any more. This may even more truthfully be said of burglaries. The old-fashioned inconvenient types of labor are going out. Especially with the daylight-saving arrangements now in vogue even the burglar can make his hay while the sun shines. He does not need to be a cracksman even; why damage the vault and perhaps the night watchman when one can enter freely by the front door when the vault is conveniently open to let out the specie and let in the office force? In short, the elements of up-to-date brigandage are now familiar to every child, while the clumsy, old-fashioned, safe-blowing, dark-lantern style of thing is left to the stage and the movies.

This phenomenon of democracy cannot be

dismissed as of no significance. It is just possible that we have overrated the rights of property. After all, why worry about mere thefts of money while the grander larcenies of air and light and cleanness, of decency, freedom, beauty, go unchallenged? It is a rough way of thinking, but there is reason in it. Democracy is vaguely unwilling to act as policeman for the rights of the few until it can protect the rights of the many, too. Meantime, the gunman who robs a bank in broad day may contribute more to the public entertainment in so doing than the less picturesque but no less predatory person who hides the sun with his smoke, smothers decency in his street cars, and blights civic beauty with his billboards, contributes to anything. Democracy will not protect such interests until they change. It vaguely feels that those lesser evils may well wait until the larger wrongs are righted, and it has a well-grounded suspicion that those who are most clamorous against the lesser wrongs are often the beneficiaries of the greater ones. Of course, this is crude and unsophisticated, but it is not wholly wrong. For the sanctions we frantically appeal to when the burglars invade our block, we really know are capable of a far wider application.

If life consists largely in emotion, as I suppose we must admit it does, how supreme among human systems must democracy appear! The feelings aroused by autocracy are puny in comparison. What passionate loyalties to persons and to parties it can evoke, potent long after elections are lost and issues dead. Think of Mr. Blaine! And what whole-hearted, ungrudging, robust hatreds, which honestly see in their object all the qualities of Judas, Lucifer, and Antichrist rolled in one! If to feel strongly is to live deeply then only in democracy is life really to be found. What passes for it elsewhere is mere pallid delusion.

In this connection it should be pointed out that in the mere matter of gloom few autocracies can compare with democracy. A few years ago all was gloom because the allies were so inconceivably blind; then because so few American soldiers were reaching France; then because it was no use anyway, for Germany could never be either starved out or worn down. After Germany finally did give way in a catastrophe that amazed even the optimists, new and greater causes for gloom disclosed themselves, in the hopeless problems raised by the winning of the war. It would almost seem that a great mistake was made in winning the war, and that it would really have been wiser to let the Germans have it.

That democracy which is neither warlike nor efficient should vanquish autocracy, which is avowedly both, is passing strange. Not less so is the humbleness of democracy, which like the apostle will not boast except of weaknesses. Democracy seems by its own account little more than a tissue of imperfections. On a recent notable literary anniversary, some of us arranged an exhibit of editions appropriate to the occasion, which in due time attracted the attention of a reporter. We imparted to him such facts as seemed suitable, and he went his way. When his paragraph appeared next morning, every several statement it contained was wrong; and yet its total impression was substantially correct. So is it with democracy. Consider it in war. Its air program falls down, its ordnance program is a failure, the soldiers do not get their mail or their pay, the Y.M.C.A. has too many meetings and too little tobacco. And yet the war is won. It makes one think of Michelangelo's Moses; there is imperfection in every detail, but the statue is sublime. In this gloomy splendor there lies democracy's hope for art, or at least the artistic temperament, which as everyone knows thrives in an atmosphere of settled despair. When is genius more productive, when it is young and desperate, or successful and middle aged? Were not Homer and Milton blind, and Dante and Hugo exiles?

This is not merely American. It is South American, British, French—in a word, it is democratic. In a measure it was Roman and Athenian in their semi-democratic days. Think of Alcibiades, Aristides, Marius and Sulla, Pompey and Caesar. And the Senate! There was a Senate even then.

In a democracy, in short, no one seems to enjoy the full popular confidence until he is dead. Safety first, you know. Indeed, it is freely alleged against democracies that they are ungrateful. They hound a man as long as he lives and then exalt him to the skies. Yet even here, where democracy is at its worst, appears again a hint of its unfathomable rightness. Leadership in democracy is a social product, and democracy instinctively recognizes it as such and refuses to be beguiled by old habits of kings and heroes into a hero worship which is out of date.

But when a great man is gone, democracy with its infallible sense of values at once seizes upon his memory and makes of him a living symbol of all the best civic elements that he embodied. Democracy was not always kind to Washington. But she has so exalted his memory that most people will not believe that he was not always the idol of his countrymen. Is this hypocrisy? Or is it a kind of deep, elemental honesty which feels that democracy is greater than its greatest individual expressions, and that it is fairly entitled to whatever symbolic value may attach to the memory of their great qualities?

Walk any pleasant evening along any important thoroughfare in the poorer part of a great city. Are not the people you meet surprisingly well dressed? You may encounter a few queer old peasants, obviously imported from an autocratic land too late for reconstruction. But most of those you see have felt the magic spell of assimilation which is the secret of democracy. Mere economists lament this, and talk of the folly of dressing beyond one's means. But the student of democracy sees in it a vast, portentous force released by democracy for the elevation of her masses. What does democracy care that you have no savings account and that you have sold your baby-bonds to buy your stylish clothes? Her only concern is that you are struggling to be like the people you consider worth while, for that ferment is worth more than thrift.

This evident disposition on the part of democracy to make itself personally presentable gives promise of a better day in city-building, of which democracy has made so dreary a business thus far. For people much concerned for their personal appearance will next be thinking of making their homes attractive, and then their streets, and then their cities. Nor will their minds, tastes, and characters escape the same strong, subtle influence. Democracy says to every man, "You can be like the best."

Democracy offers men everything. Precisely here is its tragedy. Tyranny opens to the subject no bewildering variety of possibilities. Beset by limitation, his choices are few and simple. He may live; he may be fed, clothed, and sheltered; he may even be undisturbed. If so, let him be content, and for the most part he will be. But it is the glory and the anguish of democracy that it offers the citizen everything; and he cannot possibly take it all. He is like a man let into Monte Cristo's cavern of treasure, to take away as much as he can carry. However much he may take, he will all his life lament all that he left behind.

ARCTIC VILLAGE LIFE

MALICIOUS provincials from the periphery of our country like to describe the city we inhabit as an overgrown village. I, too, think of it as the Little Village, but in affection, as Mr. Bouncer thought of London. And it is with London that our village has its chief analogies, in so far as one city may be like another.

For our village is built not like New York, upon a chain of islands, but like London, upon the land. Our Little Village is like London, too, in its cabability—that is, its inability to be navigated except by cabs. Both have parts mutually inaccessible otherwise. As in London, too, our railway stations are skilfully scattered, so that no one may thoughtlessly pass through our midst without having an opportunity to give us a few hours of his attention.

It is this location upon terra firma that enables the Little Village, like its ancient prototype, to sprawl about in all directions, and be informal and comfortable. Like London, too, it is divided by a river, which diversifies city travel with tunnels and bridges, both closed and open, and thus conserves the priceless element of adventure in our village life.

But never are we more truly the Little Village than when the snow overwhelms us and the voice of the blizzard is heard in the land. Then, indeed, we are reminded that we are geographically at least still one with the prairies about us. Time turns backward, and we experience again something of the tranquillity our childhood knew. No automobiles go by the house. Those delicate creatures are all folded soft in their comfortable garages or stalled and abandoned on distant boulevards. The sturdy and humble horse now reappears from his retirement and makes his milky way among the alleys. As in one's youth, one must go to the store for a paper, and the surest way to get one's groceries is the cash-and-carry system now advocated by economists.

The blizzard has packed the snow too hard for the snow plow and the papers call upon all public-spirited citizens to dig themselves out. "Dig a road" is the cry, and no sooner have we read it in the evening papers than my neighbors and I sally forth, man, woman, and child, and shovel snow by lamplight out of the middle of the street. In the midst of this civic carnival an automobile, one of the last of the species to penetrate these solitudes, comes sputtering along. Over our hundred feet of cleared road it bounds joyously, only to stop abruptly where our labors had ended. A youth leaps out.

"If you'd leave the darned stuff alone," he exclaims, "we'd get on all right." How patient and docile an hour's labor has made us! We gather peasant-like about him and gently point out that he hasn't any chains on. A few minutes' shoveling and a strong push from three of us rustics and he is on his way for half a block at least, leaving the fragrance of his gratitude to lighten our nocturnal toil.

The postman is now no such invisible man as Chesterton describes. He is not to be taken for granted. His occasional visits bring us news by word of mouth from the outer world. Awful things are happening. He informs us that a woman was this day overcome by cold on the street and "they brought her into the post-office and survived her." We are touched at his simple story. We are sorry about the poor woman, but if she had to go we find comfort in the fact that our postman was among those who survived her.

The situation now becomes serious. Fire engines cannot get through the snow, and fire plugs are snowed under. Milk and coal cannot be distributed.

The President calls upon students and professors to dig in a new and deeper sense, and we respond. An R.O.T.C. gentleman in khaki and puttees commands us and leads us forth by tens, shovels in hands, to our appointed block. As we go we invite recruits from our student acquaintance. We offer our patriotic example for their emulation. We wave our shovels in menace or extend them in entreaty. Our auditors are full of good intentions. They are coming out at four o'clock, or they have already been out at eleven o'clock, or this very day before breakfast did they not shovel out their sidewalk? No one joins us. We remain ten.

We reach the fatal block. The cowardly horses have evaded the drifts and broken a crooked path worthier of the wayward cow. (Can this be the etymology of "coward"?) We must hew to the line and level the drifts they have escaped. A band of schoolboys with shovels on their shoulders pass along the sidewalk. We hail them. Let them look no further. The work is here. They make light of us. They are going to an engagement. We reply that it is no crime to break an engagement, and ask them whether they are a parade or are going to have their picture taken.

They evade these questions by asking us what they hire us for and how long we have been at work. We answer, "Since five o'clock this morning."

Ten minutes have now worn away. A football youth raises the cheerful cry "Hot coffee!" as though it would come when called for, and we instinctively lift our eyes expectantly to the far end of the block. And now comes one of our colleagues, faring along the sidewalk, and we professors see our missionary opening. We offer him our shovels and a share in our civic honors.

"Hey! slacker! Come and shovel!"

He is embarrassed and begins to make excuse. He has already shoveled out his premises, and he has a department meeting at three o'clock. We show the hollowness of these pretexts, and he takes to his heels.

School is now out, and a throng of children descends upon us. One asks if we are all soldiers. Another says this is good practice for the trenches, as though we had not been describing our operations for an hour in terms of salients and traverses. A half-grown boy undertakes to boss us. We lend him a shovel and he soon grows much quieter.

Two hours have now passed. We are all much quieter. Our time is up, and we march back to headquarters to deposit our shovels. On our way we see a group of laborers digging out an alley. My colleague reflects that even in these social upheavals class distinctions persist. The high-brows do the avenues, the low-brows the streets, and the proletariat the alleys.

Going out through the falling snow to see if one could still get downtown by railway, I met our local poet and vaguely drew his attention to the enveloping element. "Beautiful snow, and all that sort of thing."

He bent a wild eye upon me. "Yes, the weather is full of literary suggestion," said he. He could have handled the storm as it was then with a slight lyrical effort, but as I look back upon it now he is in for an epic at the very least.

Arrived at the railway station, I found a train approaching, and was soon proceeding on what would in ordinary times be an express. It did, indeed, even today follow the express tracks, but halted obligingly at every possible stopping place, the natives of which might then be seen skipping across the tracks and hopping over the drifts to clamber up the steps into the train. Such deportment on the part of the inhabitants of Kenwood transcends the memory of the oldest inhabitant.

Scarcely has our community begun to resume its normal processes when another blizzard swoops down upon us. This swift succession of embarrassments fairly bowls the Little Village over. The railroads cancel their schedules. One cannot get downtown. The papers do not come. Even the telephone, the chief annoyance of civilization, is silent. Our street, usually thick with coursing motors, is for a whole day as quiet as a churchyard. All trackless lies the untrodden snow.

But when the storm is over, behold the revival with redoubled force of our new-found social spirit. It is Sunday. People going to church see the streets filled with neighbors—bankers, magnates, debutantes, and deans—shoveling out the road. The shovel suddenly becomes the badge of civic respectability. Some of us take out time to go to church, and then resume the irrepressible conflict.

A woman stops to observe us. "You ought to see our street," she remarks provocatively. We obligingly inquire as to its state.

"It was all shoveled out this morning." We express our fear that she did not go to church.

"No, indeed! We stayed home and shoveled!" she answers without contrition.

Thus does the complacency of the old ecclesiasticism give way to that of the new social religion.

A car is stalled at the corner. In sheer humanity my neighbor and I dig it out. It proceeds to his door and leaves his laundry. Assured of a clean shirt for the morrow, he exults over the ways of Providence. I cannot share his elation. Mine came the day before the blizzard.

Nothing brought home to me the extremity of the situation like seeing a policeman at work. He was shoveling snow. This happened on the eighteenth of January, 1918, at three o'clock in the afternoon. I was totally unprepared for the shock. I have seen hundreds of policemen, but I had never before seen one perform any unofficial act which might be denominated labor.

At least once a year, it is true, I have seen a policeman sell a ticket to the Policeman's Annual Benefit Ball to a man who did not want it. This is the only thing approaching an exception to the rule that I now recall. I have sometimes speculated upon the reason for this. It cannot be an accident. It is obviously a part of police punctilio.

This must remain the high point of the triumph of the storm, that it prevailed over that inexorable tradition of the Force. Such was the democratizing effect of the blizzard. One can only hope never to be called upon to witness such sights again.

Not only did we dig ourselves out. We dug out one another. Here our village consciousness showed itself. Neighborliness is not a metropolitan trait, it is a village virtue, and happily it still clings to our village. One hundred thousand strong we got out our shovels after the second snowstorm and went at our streets a block at a time. Never had our village shown its spirit more finely. The snow told us in unmistakable language what is true in a great many things besides snow, that the welfare of one depends on the welfare of all. And if these January storms really taught us this, they were worth all they cost in money, suffering, and toil.

And yet most of us, I fancy, would not for anything have missed the blizzards and the interruption of our routine, and the thrill of that great, common endeavor to clear the streets, with its good exercise in genial company and its wholesome reminder that after all we are not prim city folk, but good, old-fashioned neighbors in the greatest Little Village in the world.

A HILLTOP COLLEGE

AMONG the cultural forces powerfully at work in our college community a generation ago one of the most potent was the Greek professor's dress-suit. It was the first dress-suit most of us had ever seen. I have since seen many dress-suits, some of them splendidly worn and amply tenanted, but none has ever impressed me as did his. Our supreme social expression was the Washington Banquet, held in the parlors of the Baptist Church, and I shall never forget the sight of our professor, a fine figure of a man on all occasions, as he entered the room and moved among us clad in his dress-suit. We all felt a deep conviction that in any human society, however exalted, that figure would be at home. We instinctively recognized in him the finished man of the world. We did

not utter these convictions. They were too
universal and obvious to require expression.

I have often felt grateful to my old professor for introducing me, an impressionable
young man of fifteen, to the strange and at
first, I think it must be admitted, grotesque
sight of a dress-suit on. I do not remember
that he taught me much Greek, though he
did make me work hard, which is perhaps
not quite the same thing. But one thing he
did teach me: to look upon a dress-suit without dismay, and it is more than a jest to say
that his dress clothes were a real cultural
factor in the life of our country college. They
soundly guided our dawning social aspirations.

I cannot honestly omit from the cultural
forces of my college life my friend Clark's
tennis racquet. Clark had a tennis racquet.
I had none. Judge which of us was diligent, frugal, and industrious, and which idle,
frivolous, and given to play. But even with
the responsibilities of an upperclassman, one
must sometimes relax, and I did occasionally

borrow Clark's racquet. And all that I have since accomplished in lawn-tennis, I owe, as the oak is in the acorn, to the use I then made of that racquet. It shows what one can do, if he but apply himself, with his leisure moments, and somebody else's property—which is, if I mistake not, the foundation principle of banking.

Not that I made no return to Clark for the use of his racquet. I did make a return. It was, broadly speaking, a spiritual one, and hence difficult to set forth in precise terms. But if I explain that when I was a Senior, Clark was a Freshman, it will be realized that as he went about his work, verifying the laws of physics by observing the falling apple, or tinkering with the apparatus in the laboratory, he had the warm consciousness that his, Clark's, tennis racquet, Freshman though he was, was being used by one of those ornaments of the institution, the members of the Senior Class. It gives me pleasure to add that Clark is now president of the college, but I am not so sure he would be where he is today if I had not taken his tennis racquet off his hands at judicious intervals and thus unobtrusively kept him to his book. Such in every generation are the fatherly responsibilities of the conscientious upperclassman.

There was no low commercial instruction given in my college days, but one important way of business I did learn in my Freshman year from the village banker. He was a tall, dignified man of the old aristocratic school. He lived in a stately and beautiful old house of the southern Colonial type, with lofty Ionic pillars in front and smaller ones at either end; a house, as I lived to learn, as beautiful in its hospitality as in its architecture. And when I appeared, a Freshman, at his bank to realize on the first paternal remittance, he kindly and unforgettably showed me how to indorse a check. I can truthfully say that to this day I never pick up a check to indorse it without the stirring of some vague memory of that early lesson.

I am now able to discern with a clearness

then impossible to me the social stratification of our college community. At the top of it were the young men and women from Dayton. They enjoyed an enviable pre-eminence. We all felt that their clothes, their behavior, their savoir faire, were what everyone's ought to be. I do not mean that they put on airs. Some of them were most engagingly democratic. But so well did these young people adorn college life that we all believed that Newport, Lenox, and Bar Harbor could show them nothing. In fact, we vaguely supposed that when we withdrew for the summer vacation to the seclusion of our obscure abodes, they naturally gravitated to the seashore or the mountains. Perhaps they did. It never occurred to us to inquire. It was, at all events, the prevailing feeling of my contemporaries that the parents of these young people did the college a great service by sending them to it to leaven it with light and leading. If one of these young Olympians asked you down to visit him during spring recess, thirty years have not erased the memory; and if one of those divinely fair let her finger-tips touch yours but for one thought-less, fleeting instant, it shall never be for-gotten.

At the other extreme of our college society was a little group of youths from Chicago. We, too, were in a small way among the celebrities of the college. We were pointed to, or at, by our fellow-students, as proof of the institution's far-flung influence. It had, it appeared, been potent enough to search us out amid the rudeness and materialism of our native surroundings and draw us by its gentle influence to the college to soothe our savage breasts with learning. The only persons who in any degree disputed this distinction with us were two or three extraordinary individ-uals from the mountains of Kentucky. They and we seemed to our fellows to have come from another planet.

In the college club in which I used to board for something over two dollars a week, there sat at one end of the table a man of boundless and infectious geniality but of

Pennsylvania-Dutch extraction. At the other end sat a young German of more recent importation, a runaway scion of a Prussian Offizier-family, who after incredible hardships in German military schools had fled from what he already perceived to be Prussian tyranny. His social rating in proper German terms was quite different from that of his Pennslyvania vis-à-vis, a truth of which he was by no means unconscious. But the devastating fact was that in the no less rigid and about equally authentic social stratification of our hilltop Ohio college this rating was reversed. It meant nothing to us that our Berlin comrade could write v-o-n before his name, but it meant everything that our genial Pennsylvanian could write Phi Omicron Nu after his. In this comparative judgment the modern world has since acquiesced.

We entertained, I remember, the most extreme and lavish views as to one another's powers and prospects. It was the inward conviction of all the thoughtful men in college of my time that certain individuals would inevitably be hanged. It was not that we did not wish them well. It was only that we saw with unerring prevision what lay before them. I will not say that we were wholly wrong, but only that the moral failure of these young men has not been so marked as we then feared. For some of our contemporaries, on the other hand, we anticipated a future of extraordinary achievement. It was an open secret that one of the upperclassmen of my day knew more than the faculty. So at least his admirers said, and no one was disposed to gainsay them. We set no limit to his probable achievements. Yet he has never been greater than the day he graduated. Perhaps in outstripping the faculty he over-exerted himself. Some of our forecasts have proved more successful. The great college orator of my time was also the boxing champion. He is now a college president. Comment seems superfluous. One of my classmates early exhibited the most stupendous disposition to arrange and systematize. He even essayed to arrange the college library

[149]

and the mineral cabinet. He is now a trustee of the institution. The most desperate spirits of our day seem to have become lawyers. But so has the president of the Y.M.C.A. The general tendency of history has been to moderate rather than to negative our judgments.

Ours was a hilltop college overlooking a pleasant New England village in the Middle West. The college hill was encompassed with other hills, and it and they and the village and the four seasons, especially the spring, and the months of the year, particularly June, were perfectly smothered in poetry of our production. Even a member of the faculty now and then yielded to the spell of the place and lifted up his voice in song. There were strong Pierian elements in our college spring.

Our verse was partly humorous, sometimes didactic, but the overwhelming majority of it was sentimental. Ours were indeed Poems of Sentiment and Reflection. If one could recover a tithe of it he could pro-

duce a poetic manual completely descriptive
of that countryside. The college avenue, the
village street up and down which we deco-
rously walked half-a-dozen times a day, the
little valley which was our favorite resort in
sentimental moods, the college cemetery
where we wrote our elegies and mused con-
tentedly on the mortality of former generations—all these we celebrated in measures
only too appropriate. It was indeed the great
weakness of this literary movement that it
was if anything too correct. We said what
we expected ourselves to say, and what
earlier English poets had taught us it was
poetic to say, when confronted with a moon,
a tree, or a graveyard.

The sentiment, too, with which our measures were colored, not to say drenched, was
impeccable. Especially just after leaving college it was our wont to send back to the college paper lofty lyrics indicative of our un-
shakable attachment to its ideals, its ties, and
its surroundings. The sentiment of this later,
and as it were posthumous, poetic vintage

was even denser than that of the original output.

I cannot omit from this unconventional list of the elevating influences of my college days the village livery stable. Do not suppose that we vulgarly consorted with the stable-boys; far from it. But it was there that we procured the occasional buggies in which on balmy Saturdays in spring we traversed those pleasant roads over the hills, and conversed, or exchanged the subtler nuances of silence, with some fair companion. We had our own convictions as to the speed and endurance of the animals we drove, and engaged our favorite grays and sorrels long ahead. We knew full well how many miles beyond Alexandria or the Welsh Hills we could venture and still deliver our charges at the Seminary by supper time. For that providential practice which used to found a girls' school under the shadow of a men's college had generously placed a seminary at each end of our village street and thus brightened the student days of all of us. We used to see these bright beings from afar at church and on the main street as they and we went to and from the post-office with quite unnecessary frequency, but it was the livery, after all, which most effectually threw us together.

Since the time of Aristotle, anyway, music has been regarded as an essential part of a proper education, and of course it was included in ours. Even in my infancy I had been introduced to the fatiguing study of the piano, which I had cheerfully relinquished to take up the lighter subjects of Greek, Latin, and mathematics. In college my music was resumed, but it was no longer instrumental but vocal to which I gave myself. Not, indeed, under the direction of my professors; they took no interest in our accomplishments. It was our wont on balmy spring evenings to gather about the steps of the college building, officially known as New Brick, and lifting our young faces toward the radiant moon, to join in jocund song. The chief performer on these occasions was a gifted youth familiarly known as Gummy. His greatest musical accomplishment was his yodel, which we all firmly believed could not be surpassed by any Swiss or Tyrolese of the High Alps.

Much as we valued this nightly exercise of baying the moon in such accomplished company, it was in private from the lips of old man Brown, the mainstay of the Glee Club, that we learned those interminable darkey and student songs which informed the finished collegian of the period. And when Brown graduated and went west to teach, I found a new Mentor in the Deacon. He at last after much practice put the final indorsement upon my musical proficiency by permitting me to accompany him on his celebrated serenades, there to essay a piping obbligato to his amorous warbling. Oddly enough, both my music masters are now presidents of colleges—but not, I should add, colleges of music.

It is a strange and even a distressing thing to observe how many of the harmless, lighthearted comrades of my college days have become college presidents. In their melancholy fate I read an admonition from the oldest of schoolmasters that we are all becoming liable to the unwelcome degree of M.A., which every mature etymologist will acknowledge stands for Middle Age.

THINK, ABIB!

I RECENTLY conveyed a copy of the King James Version printed in 1611 and weighing forty pounds a distance of four hundred miles, and exhibited it for two hours in full view of an audience many of whom examined it before or after my remarks; only to read in the next morning's paper that I "insisted that the King James Version was colloquial Greek." For such gainsayings there is no sufficient answer but a line of the pungent Mr. Browning:

"Think, Abib!—Dost thou think?"

If you were born in a Mississippi River town not forty miles from the birthplace of Mark Twain, and then lived to read in a New York newspaper that not much could be expected of you in a literary way because

of your western origin, would you not wonder? Doubtless the editor had a good case,
but he chose a poor argument to support it.
I think little of aetiology, but if we must be
aetiologists, and estimate everything by its
source, then let us be so in good earnest.

And when you read in a metropolitan
editorial that "If Christ Came to Chicago"
was written by a Middle Western clergyman,
instead of by W. T. Stead, the father of modern journalism, again you find solace in Mr.
Browning. And you are tempted to exclaim
with the modern psalmist, "Lord! What do
they understand?"

In a state the name of which would surprise no one, on election-day a certain political group invaded the stronghold of another, with casualties to the number of four
dead and seventeen wounded. The authorities became interested, whereupon all concerned in the shooting (excepting four, of
course) addressed a petition to the county
judge and the state's attorney, stating that
they "failed to see how any good could re-

sult from litigation over the matter," and expressing their willingness to "let bygones be bygones." To ask these petitioners to think would clearly be too much. Let us rather say, "Smile, Abib!—Canst thou smile?"

But, after all, why should anyone think when there are so many convenient and amusing substitutes for thought? Such as reading, or letting someone else do your thinking for you. Then there is the questionnaire, by the aid of which you can so quickly assemble a huge mass of statistics, or husks of thought, by which the craving for it may for a time be appeased. The card catalogue is another good substitute, and so is the use of different colors of paper for your notes. There is also the filing system and the radio. These devices and many more occupy our hands and eyes and attention as we potter about the brink of thought and occasionally dip a hesitating foot in its forbidding waters.

A seasoned colleague assures me that this is the one thing students refuse to do. They will come regularly, listen patiently, take notes diligently, read ravenously, compose voluminously—do everything, in short, but think. Ask whatever else, and they will dare, but never, ah never, require of them the dread adventure of independent thought! From it, they instinctively feel, they might perhaps never return.

For my part, I am skeptical about this. But there is no doubt that nothing so bewilders the student as to see a professor think. A great chemist of my acquaintance has been known to stop and actually think right before his class for as much as two or even three minutes. Picture the scene! The Man of Science momentarily silent, a faraway look in his eyes; about him his devoted students, awestruck and even a little alarmed at the consciousness that the sublime processes of thought are actually going on before them, and haunted by a vague apprehension that their yogi may never emerge from his absorption.

But few people have the courage of the great chemist. For to have to stop and think

is generally regarded as a sure token of intellectual bankruptcy. "He didn't know
what to say; he had to stop and think!" is a
common formula of failure. Only with great
reluctance do we look into the recesses of our
minds, fearful of what we may find, or fail
to find, there, and to have to do it is generally recognized as a last desperate resort. If
words fail you, then, and then only, have
recourse to thought.

For words have somehow taken the place
of thought. From being its expression they
have become its substitute, until an old
thought put in new words strikes the mind
as something revolutionary. Which may remind us of the final inadequacy of words fully
to express thought. Not for nothing do we
speak of reducing a thought to writing.
Writing does reduce it, beyond question, as a
photograph reduces a landscape. Thought
like feeling is too much for the resources of
language.

It is instructive to observe how even a
thought once formulated will ride down the

stream of time long after its inner vitality has departed. Like the buttons on the back of a frock coat, they persist among us even when their usefulness has ceased. Laws, institutions, clubs, habits, causes, all occasionally fall under this condemnation.

Of course, language is sometimes ambiguous, and the thoughts we elicit from others may be quite different from those we intend. A physicist, having asked his class in what three states matter is found, is surprised to learn that one pupil has found it principally in Alabama, Pennsylvania, and Michigan. Upon further inquiring the difference between a red light and a green one, he is informed that a red light means "Stop," and a green one "Go ahead." Which reminds you of asking a group of youths the meaning of ochre, whereon one declared it to be a game; another a cruel monster, and a third a vegetable. All these answers reflect processes of thought, though not precisely the one the instructor in his blindness had foreseen.

THINGS SEEN AND HEARD

If thought be the perception of relations
between things known, it is plain that things
must first be known in order to be thought
about. When such mental possessions are so
few and scattered that the mind cannot see
from one to another, thought is impossible.
It is difficult really to think about a single
thing; like erecting a bridge upon a single
point.

It is just here that ignorance becomes a
positive obstacle to thought. And so it
comes about that many excellent people who
have not mental possessions enough to justify setting up lines of communication between
them fall back upon their emotions and feel
instead of thinking. There is of course not the
slightest harm in this, so long as they know
what they are doing. The trouble is they
usually do not know they are feeling, and
actually suppose they are thinking.

But the truth is, the absence of information is less annoying and perilous than its
too sudden acquisition. As Epictetus put it,
"Where did you so suddenly learn wisdom?"

THINK, ABIB!

From the times of Thackeray and Molière much obliquy has been heaped upon the *Nouveau Riche* and his behavior. But little has been said on the far larger subject of the *Nouveau Sage*. That a little knowledge is a dangerous thing has long been recognized; but the truth is, a great deal of it may be something worse than dangerous. It is not the size but the suddenness of the transition that dizzies him who makes it. And to one who has known a thing for a long time no one is so offensive as one who is puffed up over just having learned it.

In days now best forgotten I spent an afternoon on the drill ground mastering what is known as "squads right." That intricate evolution is nothing less than the essential unit of martial science. It is the atom of the military universe. Did it cease to function, the most colossal strategy were vain. Yet tacticians make little of it, so confidently do they count on its stability.

It is no small thing to learn nevertheless, and we went home from drill that evening weary but triumphant. We had painfully and laboriously mastered the maneuver, and looked forward with real pleasure to performing it the next day. But on that day to our intense annoyance appeared a distinguished colleague who had missed the previous day's drill, and had to be put through it, and the whole afternoon was spent by our officer and the entire squad in imparting the necessary mystery to him. And how slowly he absorbed it! It seemed to all us recent initiates that the man was impossibly and incredibly dull. Really, he did not seem to know his right hand, or at least foot, from his left. All the afternoon we stumbled after, over, and around him, and at last about sunset our labors were rewarded, and he could do it too.

This memory should make us kindly disposed toward the newly wise. For after all we had learned it only twenty-four hours sooner. But what a colossal sense of superiority it gave us! A start of twenty-four hours! What is it? Well, psychologically everything! Why, to arrive at truth a few minutes or even seconds ahead of you may become the ground of extravagant self-felicitations on the part of your nearest and dearest.

The traveler to antique lands or even to distant parts of our own brings back rare articles of vocabulary with which to delight and amaze his simple neighbors. Mere names of unheard-of mountains, lakes, or rivers, pronounced if possible in the local manner, will do much in that direction, but there is nothing like an occasional phrase of Bantu or Swahili brought into the conversation at intervals in a thoroughly offhand manner and when least expected.

An accomplished chauffeur of my acquaintance occasionally makes full use of his mind, with surprising results. Being satisfied, as most people are, that the climate is changing, he cast about for an explanation for it, and soon found it in the recent development of radio with its attendant static. A professor with more knowledge and perhaps less imagination was at once consulted, but not convinced.

To know, and yet to think; that is the problem. For knowledge conventionally held too often admits only conventional habits of thought and leaves no room for its rightful freedom and audacity. Tame thought, like the caged condor, is a sad spectacle, stripped of its power, originality, and daring.

Some people are too well bred to think, and are content to repeat polite formulas of thought. Yet without going so far as to seem rash or ill mannered, we can all use our minds a little more and our memories a little less, and we would all of us do well to indulge much more freely in the luxury of independent thought.

On a certain Sunday afternoon a year or two ago a little group of white-faced men sat huddled on the stage of a downtown theater, gazing into the expectant faces of a great audience. It was the birthday of Copernicus. Few men have done a more daring piece of thinking for our unthinking race than he.

THINK, ABIB!

To rethink the arrangement of the solar system within the narrow limits of one small head was a prodigious achievement, and on a stage set with the insubstantial scenery of "Shuffle Along" we were to interpret his significance in the history of human thought.

Our subject was certainly in glaring contrast with our setting. But, after all, few human performances can boast a proper background. If we waited for that, the play would never begin. And many a very pretty human stage accommodates a show not half good enough for it. How few great houses have witnessed great actions! Some are famous because Queen Elizabeth slept in them. It was the best she could do. It is to the cottages and the mangers that our pilgrimages chiefly take us. It is on Main Street, not on Fifth Avenue, that life likes to stage its choicest efforts. Of course, this is not the way we would do these things, but the gods think differently.

Thus against the flimsy background of

reality the human spirit works out its immortal business, *sub specie aeternitatis*.

But the business of thinking cannot be left altogether to Galileo and Copernicus. Abib must do his share. Even if he have no such massive ideas to deal with, let him whet his wits upon the subject matter of daily life. "It is amusing," said the great Erasmus, "to deal with trifles in such a way as to show one's self anything but a trifler." And only so shall we be ready to understand and follow Copernicus when he appears. This is what leads to martyrdoms; a great thinker in the midst of an unthinking mass. Of course, they always kill him, in one way or another. What else is there for them to do? They cannot understand him, for they are completely out of the habit of thought, and in so doing they only defeat themselves. It is not for lack of leadership that society languishes, but for the individual's reluctance to do his just share of the world's thinking, in effect demanding that another, whom he will lazily declare more gifted than himself, must drag him on. As one looks about him, the whole situation, religious, political, and industrial, seems but a sermon on this text.

It was thinking upon them that struck the deathblow at dueling and slavery, not so very long ago, when those practices had what seemed to almost everybody an impregnable position in modern life. But a few men began to think, and to think differently, and now everyone agrees with them. And those were not the only practices in human society worth thinking about. Yet some very important people have got so in the habit of thinking what people expect them to think that no other kind of thought is possible for them any more.

There is one great disadvantage about printing, that it tends to make us indolent in thought, for it makes it so much easier to get our thoughts ready-made. It is doubtful whether the loud and confident reiteration of other people's thoughts, usually unverified and hardly even understood, was ever more general. Which makes Mr. Browning's invitation more than ever timely now.

THE SELF-MADE ARTICLE

THERE come times in the lives of not a few of us when we cry out with the satirist, "Semper auditor ego?" "Must I always listen?" and we write an article. It might be truer to say that it writes itself, for there is a kind of prophetic burden about it that leaves us no peace until it is off our minds. We are undoubtedly better, and for the time being happier, men for having written it.

Upon the exhilaration of this creative act, however, presently ensues a period of depression. For what is to be done with the article? It was indeed much to write it; but surely that is not enough. Others should see it and profit by it. If it was good for you to write it, how much better for them to read it. Obviously, it must be published.

THE SELF-MADE ARTICLE

Of course, I do not refer to those lifeless productions manufactured to order upon lines laid down by some overshadowing editorial patron, who tells you what he wants you to write about, and at what length. I have in mind the spontaneous, involuntary, self-made article, which writes itself in accordance with the doctrine of predestination, and has in consequence its own way to make in a cold and calculating world.

You will of course take stock of such editors as you can think of, and wonder which of them, if any, is wise and great enough to perceive the worth of your article, and, putting all lesser articles aside, to cleave only unto it for his next number. To him then, in a letter studiously disinterested, you presently offer the signal opportunity. You do not urge nor flatter. You address him with a reserve comporting with the dignity of the transaction. For you are offering him not a bench or a boot that you have made, but a fragment of your personality. You are asking him to become the guardian of your child. And you have an inward conviction that it is not you but he who is to have judgment passed upon him in his decision. When he thinks that he is answering, "This is not good enough for me," he will in effect be saying, "I am not good enough for this."

It is said that in the West Indies they catch a variety of fish which at certain seasons is very poisonous but at other times is perfectly edible. The test is to drop a silver coin into the pot while the fish is boiling. If it turn black there is death in the pot; the fish cannot be eaten. So with your article. When you have caught your idea and have it well a-stewing, cast in your editor. If he turn black, what you have is but a deadly mess; but if he keep his fine, silvery color, your dish is fit for public consumption.

But what a singular being is an editor! I have seen one praise an article more in refusing it than he would another in accepting it. Of what does this convict him? Is it not unscrupulous thus to accept the worse and refuse the better? Is he merely being over-

charitable? Or are some contributions in very
sooth too good to print, and must the practical editor bow to the mandate of his de-
praved public? I do not know. There are
doubtless polite or pious fictions in all pro-
fessions.

I have myself sat in the seat of the scorn-
ful in my time, and with Olympian serenity
accepted and refused articles. Whom I would
I slew, and whom I would I left alive. And I
know full well the bewildering variety of
pretexts to which editors will resort in their
extremity. As, that they have already accepted an article on a similar subject. Yet
you look month after month for the similar
article in vain; it never appears. Or, that
the printers' strike makes it impossible for
them to accept any more articles with even
the remotest prospect of publication.

Why do not editors tell us bluntly and
frankly the simple truth, that the self-made
article is not good enough? Why do they resort to these pitiable subterfuges of "strikes"
and "similar articles" and I know not what

besides? Perhaps from tenderness of heart; they would not hurt our feelings. But sometimes, I am sure, this indirectness is due to a haunting apprehension that some day you may produce something that will print, and then you will turn on the too-candid refuser of your earlier efforts and pillory him as one who did not know genius when he saw it and vainly strove to keep a good man down. Some such bitter experience back in the early ages of editorial evolution must explain the instinctive self-protection characteristic of the modern editor.

Yet we must all bear with his refusals now and then, for the truth is, everybody is writing for the magazines. With one-third of your subscribers offering you articles in a single year, what are you to do? In three years you may expect to hear articularly from your whole subscribing public. That fine old docile figure, the inarticulate subscriber, is no more.

Of course, not all of this proffered literature can actually be printed in the magazine.

THE SELF-MADE ARTICLE

But that is a detail. The all-important fact is that we are all writing for it. And with all the editor's threadbare excuses for sending back our lucubrations, as he all but invariably does, how enormously it must buoy him up to feel that we are all, to the last man, woman, and child, back of him. His magazine cannot fail with such a clientèle of rising authorship. He has but to take fortune at the flood and let us all together bear him on to success. Makeup day can never catch him unprepared so long as we, with untiring diligence, keep the office stocked with six hundred freshly volunteered articles a week, or enough to fill the magazine for three solid years. What if all his professional writers, wickedly covetous of five cents a word, strike and abandon him? We will not let him fail, but will rise in our awful might and throw into the scale the enormous weight of the self-made article.

Hysterical persons frequently inquire what we are coming to. In literature, at least, the answer is easy: democratization. Once few read and fewer wrote. But the monopoly of our spirits by those dead but sceptered sovereigns is done for. Soon all will read and all write. And this will be no sham democracy in which grown-ups write for helpless childhood. A day of vengeance has come in these matters, and now children write for grown-ups, and the grown-ups have to read it, for everyone else does, and grown-ups of all people can least afford to be left behind.

One thing and one only stands in the way: the cost of printing. It is coming to be about as expensive to publish a book in print as it was in olden time to publish it (in a smaller edition) in manuscript. But what good books men had to write then to get them published—Iliads and Aeneids and Divine Comedies. Printing costs may yet justify themselves by the salutary selective influence they exercise upon literature.

But that millennial dawn when all the articles of all of us will be accepted is still far away. Today almost as many come back as go forth. Like the stars, not one of them is missing. With what dismay you behold the unmistakable long envelope projecting from the postman's paw as he comes up the walk. After such a desolating moment it is at least fitting to permit an interval—a period of mourning, as it were—to elapse before offering another article, and thus turning your cheek to the smiter—no inappropriate figure, I submit, from either point of view. And when your friends inquire solicitously when your next article is coming out, you simply cannot disclose to them the fatal packet which is even now hidden beneath your cloak like the Spartan's wolf, and similarly occupied.

The world is full of magazines and journals of many descriptions, but there is one of extraordinary promise of success that does not, I believe, exist: the Magazine of Rejected Manuscripts. What a host of contributors would be at once available to crowd its pages. Not all of them indeed distinguished, yet indubitably including in their ranks the literary celebrities of the future, and probably all such celebrities, for who that ever arrived in literature had all his contributions accepted from the first? Many a heart is caught on the rebound, and many a very pretty article that has found its first editorial reader in an indigestive mood would be available for the new journal. And what a host of subscribers it would have! A mighty army of prospective contributors would spring up in a single night to form its subscription list. Nor could the general public stand coldly aloof from the only unique magazine on earth. Curiosity would advertise it throughout the land, and a nation of readers would pluck it from the news-stands, palpitating to learn at last what the oligarchy of editors has so long striven to keep from them. There would be something irresistibly comprehensive, democratic, and hospitable about such a publication. It would so palpably exemplify in literature the great Anglo-Saxon principle of Free Speech.

We might not all, indeed, live to see our contributions appear in its beneficent pages, for of course it would be overwhelmed with material from the start. But we should have at least the soothing sense, even in the hour of dissolution, that if the universe continued to hold together, they would in the course of time be posthumously produced in print.

Above all, how easily and amiably would such a magazine be edited! The editor would require only the written rejection of the article in question by any other known editor, and he would, *ex hypothesi*, accept it without parley. He would not even have to read it over, that having been done (presumably) by the rejecting editor. His rule and canon would be, "If it is bad enough for any other editor to refuse, it is good enough for me to print." This would insure the human and really representative character of the Magazine of Rejected Manuscripts. In it the vast, inarticulate majority of patient, sorely tried readers, old men and maidens and little children, the submerged ninety-nine per cent of mankind, who read on and on without being able to lift a pen in self-

[179]

defense, would come at last into their own.

In Utopia—perhaps already in Bolshevi-kia—such a magazine must exist. But in our present materialistic civilization the unique distinction about authorship is that it involves proficiency in two widely separated arts: the art of writing and the art of selling. You must market your product. I read few articles without admiration, but it is sometimes less for them as literary achievements than as triumphs of salesmanship.

ORGANIZED CURIOSITY

AS one surveys the conversational cosmos he is tempted to exclaim, "How much better is a sheep than a man!" It is difficult to be waspish or insinuating when one's vocabulary is limited to the mono-syllable "Ba," although man has made even that essentially good-natured and harmless word a vehicle of contempt. It is true the gifted and interesting cat can impart an in-finite variety of expression to her meager vocabulary, and she and her family can make the most annoying faces at the objects of their dislike. But animal-kind, in general, has to resort to overt violence if it wishes to be disagreeable. It cannot even tell a lie.

Over against this amiable background what a thing is man! He (or she) can swing in a hammock looking like an angel and watching the fleecy clouds, and tranquilly say things that will madden you. He can blast your hopes, murder your affections, and poison your soul, simply by manipulating his lips and tongue. He does not even have to raise his voice or make a face. Such is the power of speech. I know that language is immeasurably the greatest of human inventions. Of course it has its uses. But just as certainly it is responsible for most of this world's woe.

Out of these profound reflections rises the query, Would we be better off dumb? Or if not, what is the justification of speech? What good can it show to offset this immeasurable harm? What is its right to be?

You sometimes hear people say, "If I couldn't talk about it, I should burst!" Here is the answer. Speech is the exhaust. Without it we should burst daily. It is the escapement. It must not be taken too seriously. Few mean all they say. Their nervous systems are just getting their balance by letting off a little pent-up energy in talk. Who does not feel better after sputtering a bit? It is usually supposed that man invented speech to communicate ideas. I venture to deny this. He did it to relieve his feelings. Which should make us newly pitiful to all dumb creatures.

Beyond all doubt this is the rationale of the questionnaire. A group of restless spirits being assembled together cast about for a vent for their waste energy. Even conversation fails; each already knows all the others have to say. To question one another would be absurd. They therefore direct their interrogations into the air, conceiving them as addressed to vague, distant figures, who may not even exist, for all they know. Off goes a questionnaire, and they experience immediate and complete relief. Returns do not matter in the least. Everyone knows that the one unimportant thing about a questionnaire is the answers to it. Of course, hyperconscientious individuals like you and me spend hours guessing out the answers to these creations of idle fancy, but in our hearts we know that the indefatigable minds that

[183]

framed these inquiries have forgotten them already.

The questionnaire is apparently of royal origin. The first one known seems to have been sent by the king of Syria to the king of Israel, and it called forth a classic retort, which should be written at the head of every response to one, "Consider, I pray you, and see how he seeketh a quarrel against me!" It is one of the perversities of human history that this essentially autocratic institution has revived in a supposedly democratic age. For just as the eighteenth century witnessed the perfection of *La Guillotine*, the twentieth has seen that of an instrument more dreadful, if less sanguinary, *La Questionnaire*.

There are questionnaires short and questionnaires long. Beyond doubt, the latter are the more dreadful, but the short ones, too, sometimes make flattering demands upon one's powers. You are asked to send a western correspondent your latest faculty list, checking on it the positions that are vacant this year "and those that are to be

vacant next year." You are complimented
no doubt, but you feel like rending your
clothes and exclaiming with an earlier recipient, "Am I God that this man doth send unto me?" Only the modern questionnaire is
not ordinarily accompanied with six thousand pieces of gold and ten changes of rai-
ment. You are, in fact, fortunate if its gifted
senders inclose a stamp, but they do invariably "thank you in advance" for your reply.

The questionnaire is not the only modern
device for arriving at knowledge without
threading the dusty paths of toil. The Ouija
board is another. Of course those who worship Ouija will think this a flippant and sac-
rilegious remark; and so will those who worship Questionnaire. But is it not true that
even as the unsophisticated when in doubt
have recourse to the Ouija board, the intellectual take refuge in the questionnaire?

It may seem to some that Ouija is inter-
rogated upon a wider range of topics than
Questionnaire, but this is doubtful. The
questionnaire serves an amazing variety of

uses, or at least purposes. I have shown how it may be used to forecast the future. But it may be turned with equal success upon the past. I recently expended myself upon answering one of middling length—a preamble and six questions—the first being, "Is the above the proper explanation of the Greek text? If so, why so? If not, why not?" The inquirer was a lawyer. I hope he won his case. I certainly did my best for him.

Psychologists derive great happiness from propounding questionnaires, and bring up their students to do so. If a professor can secure material for lectures and articles by scattering questionnaires o'er a smiling land, observing students can get you and me to write their term papers for them in like manner. Decorous ladies in attendance upon a philanthropic tea have thrust into their hands by an eager student a list of twenty questions, some with twelve subheads, to answer on the spot about their hopes, fears, aims, thoughts, occupations, and experiences, not forgetting such inflammatory inquiries as "Do you think women have a fair chance in life? Why?"

An aspirant in business psychology, a complete stranger, thus mimeographically addresses you: "What is your opinion of the economic wisdom of university professors' purchasing jointly with other tenants the flat-buildings in which they reside? Should this be done only when there are enough purchasers to occupy all the flats? If not, what proportion of purchasers to flats would you consider reasonable? Give the reasons for your views." This poor young man did not live to enjoy my reasoned observations on this absorbing subject, for I have never heard from him since, and in view of his unmistakable interest in my economic welfare, he would hardly have failed to continue an acquaintance he himself had sought.

I would not be misunderstood. I am both professionally and temperamentally addicted to imparting information, and I would willingly labor from dawn until dark guessing out the answers to these ingenious queries, if that were what was wanted. But it is not. What is wanted is a statistic. My labored contribution, painstakingly worked out with much consultation of reports and monographs, will in the end make a difference of perhaps point two in a finding running much as follows: "Your Committee K begs leave to report that sixty-three mimeographed copies of Questionnaire No. 19A were sent out to a representative list of persons chosen entirely at random. Of these nine, or fourteen and two-sevenths per cent, were returned marked 'Cannot be delivered.' Of the remaining fifty-four, eighteen, or thirty-three and one-third per cent, have not been returned in time for use in this report," and so forth.

This, if you ever hear of it, may lead you to wonder whether the first nine, who had the wisdom to hide themselves in the day of visitation, had not chosen the better part. But you will not hear. No one does. Of the questionnaires near and far to which I have made my offering as solicited, I have been sent the upshot of but one, and that was from Texas years ago, before the technique of the thing had reached its present perfection. You do not even know whether the thing has ever reached Committee K, unless the chairman writes you to say that it has not. Then you know.

I would rise to propose that it be made the law of the land that every contributor to any questionnaire whatsoever receive one copy of the report, findings, or upshot based on his and all other such answers, within one year from the date of writing and without expense. Even if one cares nothing about the subject per se, yet by the time one has labored over it for an hour or two, one's interest is inevitably aroused in it as a sporting proposition, and one cannot help wondering whether he has put his money on the wrong horse.

Of course, it does not altogether escape you that what is really being studied in these intimate inquiries about flats and a fair chance in life is not the subject, but the answerer. You are the curious specimen upon whom the microscope is being turned, and you are being scrutinized, as in a slide, wriggling and twisting before the delighted but impartial eye of observation. And it is you and your "behavior" that they will later judge and classify, and file away in the dust among their precious "materials." But no one can begrudge you a hurried and not unrevealing return glance at the glowering orb above mentioned, before you are whisked out of the field to make room for another specimen. And does not every subtle question seem to look loftily down at you and say, "Ha! Look at me, my friend! Did you ever think of that before?"

The friend in Texas, by the way, deserves the passing tribute of a sigh. He was of a nobler disposition than most persons similarly addicted, but he was evil starred. With the amount of zeal usual with the profession, he drew his bow at a venture and addressed among others no less a personage than the Bishop of Durham. The bishop obligingly replied, but bewildered his interrogator by signing himself by a name known neither in heaven or earth—Dunelm. He signed it, moreover, with a careless elegance which led our friend to decipher it "Dunehm." He had hoped for a weighty scholastic authority, and behold he drew from out the void this less than human thing. How could he know that time out of mind the bishops of Durham have thus quaintly disguised themselves with the Latin epithet reminiscent of ancient Dunholme, and conveniently abbreviated? But "Fear not to touch the best" has ever been the questioner's motto. Did not the first one begin upon a king?

The Bishop of Gloucester answered with equal politeness and self-effacement, reducing our poor interrogator to the desolating admission, "I cannot decipher his name." Truly their sorrows shall be multiplied who seek after bishops, with the covert intention of harnessing them up to a questionnaire.

But let us be just. I confess to a certain thrill of joy at the sight of each new questionnaire, and though I count that day lost which does not bring two fresh ones under my observation, I own I open each one with more curiosity than I feel for the morning paper. "What will they be after asking now?" I say to myself, and I am seldom disappointed.

How flattering to be asked, "as a man of discression," as one questioner puts it, how many acres there should be in a college campus, and how many buildings per acre!

How refreshing to be called upon to state the number of members in the German Reichstag, and above all to reveal that most esoteric mystery, the exact post-office address of the former Kaiser! One is reminded of being asked, amid a string of similar inquiries, what verse of Ecclesiastes expresses the theme of the Iliad—clearly a problem with two unknown quantities, leaving one in doubt whether first to read the epic in question to find out its theme, or to read the Scripture in the hope of chancing upon the suitable verse.

ORGANIZED CURIOSITY

It is at least evident that much information may be gratuitously secured by this simple device, upon economics, religion, education, psychology, history, politics, and other subjects, not to mention the future and the past. I do not say that the use of the questionnaire has gone too far. It has hardly begun. I can see much further development before it. Why should anyone in need of legal advice resort to the precarious method of engaging some eminent practitioner in casual conversation on the suburban platform, and incidentally bringing up the subject, still less of going out and hiring a lawyer? All that is necessary is to send out a short questionnaire to a dozen or twenty leaders of the American bar, being careful to append to each the searching words of my own legal inquirer, "If so, why so? If not, why not?" When the answers are all in, a few minutes' computation should lead to valuable results. If Galileo had only thought to issue a questionnaire on the movement of the earth and other problems that disturbed him, how different the history of modern science might have been!

I have little patience, however, with mere cynical divagations unrelieved by practical suggestion. What is to be the outcome of this extraordinary recrudescence of the venerable questionnaire? A new vocation is to emerge. I am more and more convinced that we are to witness an addition to Mr. Chesterton's Queer Trades. For as the moon will draw the sea, the questionnaire will have its answerer.

Let it not be carelessly assumed that anybody can do this. There is a technique in answering these affairs just as surely as there is in contriving them. I observe in myself a growing facility in distributing precise answers—"Yes," "No," "Yes and No," "I have no means of knowing," and the like—judiciously among the dotted lines so generously provided. But of course a professionally trained expert with a World's Almanac and a running hand could answer them in half the time.

ORGANIZED CURIOSITY

Some people fear to prophesy, but I have answered too many forward-looking questionnaires for that, and the time is coming when every institution must have an encyclopedic authority solely concerned with answering these questions, if what Mr. Bentley calls the spirit of aimless inquiry prevailing in this restless day is to be satisfied.

No one should lose a questionnaire. At no distant day museums will be provided for their accommodation, and a mellow archaeological radiance will cluster round these quaint devices for sounding the shallows of truth.

And finally, when the new profession is scientifically equipped and the museum material is of sufficient bulk, we shall have the satisfaction of subjecting the questionnaire and its creators to a rigorous scientific scrutiny. The worm will turn. We shall reverse the microscope and from its lower end glower back upon our self constituted investigators. Every questionnaire that flutters down like autumn leaves upon our desk will at once be assigned to its proper place in the new ology. By turning to an alphabetical filing case close at hand the answers to all their supposedly novel inquiries will at once be found. The character, motives, indirections, and carefully hidden weaknesses of its mysterious perpetrators will be revealed, and we shall return to them not only the obvious answers to their easy questions, but an impartial and benevolent diagnosis of their psychological symptoms with some simple remedies sure to be within the reach of all and likely to produce a permanent cure.

THE WEEK-ENDER

IN the times of Henry VII, the story runs, there lived in Swaffham Market, in Norfolk, a peddler named John Chapman. Having dreamed one night that, if he went up to London, on London Bridge he would meet a man who would bring him good news, and being unable to get this dream out of his mind, he presently betook himself to London, and all day long walked to and fro on London Bridge. At length a shopkeeper, noting his strange behavior, asked him the meaning of it, and the honest peddler told him his dream.

"Ah!" said the shopkeeper, "had I taken account of dreams, I might have seemed as much a fool as you; for only the other night I dreamed that in a place called Swaffham Market, in Norfolk, there lives a peddler named John Chapman, who has a tree in his backside, under which is buried a pot of gold."

The peddler humbly acknowledged the folly of such behavior and forthwith returned home. There he lost no time in digging under the tree in his backside, and in very truth found just such a pot of gold as the shopkeeper had dreamed of, whereby he lived in plenty the rest of his days.

It must be evident that, under some subtle influence—a dream, an invitation, or a prospectus—John Chapman went off for a week-end, and came back from it with his eyes opened to new possibilities at home. Every week-ender knows that many a problem insoluble on a Friday will yield to treatment on a Tuesday.

Just as the provincial peddler turned for his holiday to the metropolis, the metropolite naturally seeks his in remote rural solitude. It is my hard lot to spend a part of my summer breadwinning in the stifling city, and to have only the week-ends with my family in the country. Between the scene of my labors and the bosky isle which they inhabit lie four hundred miles of rail, with which my weekly journeys have now made me reasonably familiar. And what with four days and three nights in town, and four nights and three days out of it, I sometimes hardly know which is the week and which the week-end.

I write this memoir on the way back from one of these tranquil retreats from the bustling world. This morning I did nothing at all that I remember, except rise at six, help anchor and beflag the stake-boat and the finish-boat for a regatta, act as announcer for the opening events, drive a launch in the procession, compete in a boat-race, and paddle violently in three hot canoe-dashes, besides communing with nature in the intervals. We had just time for lunch before I left for the train; and now, rested and refreshed, I am returning to the busy city, eager to participate again in its fervid life.

It is no great inconvenience for the island

household to have me ply between it and the marts of trade, and I sometimes prove very useful indeed as a sort of pony express. Week-enders, I believe, always carry candy, melons, or green corn; but my supreme exploit in transportation was the night I staggered backward off the steps of a moving station bus, with a large suitcase, a box of candy, and a seven-foot beach umbrella in my otherwise empty hands. Of course, I added a basket of fruit before venturing on the train. John Chapman himself can hardly have returned from London heavier laden.

I went week-ending once in Egypt, years ago, with a plum cake, and a basket of vegetables—the leeks and onions of Egypt—so huge that it and I occupied an entire compartment of the Fayum train. Something like this happened last summer, when I was escorting north a wooden ash-stand perhaps two feet high, in the form of a negro waiter. The person who sold him to me asked me where he was to stand; and when I said on the porch of a summer cottage, she answered brightly, "Then this will be just the thing. You know you want a touch of color." But when packed and boxed, my touch of color proved too bulky to go under the berth, nor could his congener, the porter, find room for him in his closet or in the vestibule; and in the end he did in simple fact occupy an upper all by himself, even as I.

Why is it that the week-ender, no matter how high minded, thus unfailingly degenerates into a beast of burden? Are there not express companies and parcel posts? Yet who cares for what they bring? A commonplace-looking bundle is pushed at you over the post-office counter: it must be those bathing-shoes come at last, when the interest felt in ordering them has evaporated. But to arrive at the island before breakfast, bringing out of one's pack things ordered, or, better, unexpected—this has about it something of Santa Claus and the Swaffham peddler combined. The things you bring are the spoils of your hunting; you have somehow wrung them out of the vast, impersonal city, and you come bringing them in an elemental sort of triumph. Your arrival becomes an event.

There is also another reason for this pack-horse phase of week-ending: you forgot to get the things until the last minute, and you had to carry them, or arrive ingloriously, bringing nothing more welcome or substantial than explanations. Besides, shopping for the paraphernalia of sport through the week helps to keep one in a holiday frame of mind. And was not John Chapman, that patron of week-enders, himself a peddler by profession?

The beach umbrella was for the Fourth of July; but lesser occasions, like regattas, have their uses for the week-end express. All I brought up last Friday night, that I now recall, besides my personal luggage, was two paddles, three boxes of candy, a boat-hook, a navy anchor, and six rope fenders for the launch. The boat-hook, I remember (someone else won it and now rejoices in it), was of a peculiar elegance, being tipped with brass. As I was buying it in a sporting-goods store, a boy and a man looked on. "We

ought to have one of those," said the boy,
and added with fine inconsequence, "What's
it for?" "It's to open and close windows
with," said the man; thus betraying his narrow urban horizon.

The picturesqueness of our island remote-
ness is accentuated by the railway which con-
nects us with the great world. For more than
twenty years it has stood like a rock against
the encroachments of fashion and our too
mechanical age. On it one finds none of the
freakish contrivances of modern travel. Its
fine old sleepers go back to the Victorian
period. I have made some study of archae-
ology, but I must confess that in the dim
pillared aisles of some of these ancient coach-
es I stand in awe, not to say dread. What
wassail of thirsty fishing-clubs have these
venerable vehicles not witnessed! They are
as redolent of antiquity as Dickens' ghostly
stage-coaches, only these hoary conveyances
are still awheel. The porters are of an appropriate maturity. They are like old family servants. The same old darky year after

year greets you at the steps of your Pullman, and the dining-car conductors are old family friends, to whom fathers introduce their children.

The locomotives, too, have their distinctive traits. Most engines start slowly and reluctantly, but in this ozone-laden air, the very engines jump forward eagerly to their task, and the whole train starts with a thrilling jerk. Strangers misunderstand this, but the sympathetic and reflective week-ender sees deeper into it, and comes to find the lazy ways of city locomotives tedious and annoying by contrast. It is an experience to see one of these quaint engines, with its spark-arrester, so suggestive of afternoon tea, jauntily perched upon its smokestack, ricocheting along the rails, or, in more pensive mood, stealthily pushing its way through the thick shrubbery that overhangs the track. Our railroad has a system of powerful locomotives, each eighty cubits long and capable of six thousand horse-power. But it has never profaned our forest solitudes by the admission of these monsters. They would wreck the mossy old bridges, frighten the timid creatures of the wood, and put the wayside golfer off his game.

But what a thing it is, in the dewy freshness of early morning, having again survived the perils of travel, to descend from the train upon the very shores of a certain friendly lake! The launches from the scattered cottages that dot the points and islands are picturesquely clustered at the landing just beyond the trees. In a moment they are filled and scatter, and proud is he who gets away first with his load. In a minute or two they are strung out in a gallant line, making each for his particular breakfast-table, about which will soon gather the gayest breakfast-party of the week. News of the city and the lake will be exchanged, and plans discussed for the three days that make up a proper week-end. It is now that the week-ender opens his capacious pack and draws out a new rug for the living-room and a six-foot flag to fly in the regatta. He has also a new fire-screen, a can of paint for the boathouse, and a pair of wading boots for the general good. Of a truth, there is no morning like Saturday morning, and the week-ender is its prophet.

If it be true that habitual week-ending imparts to existence a hectic hue (and hectic, if I remember, began by meaning habitual), it has its sanative properties as well. There is nothing like a change of air, and to change it twice a week all summer should restore any appetite. How much the stable native population which ministers to our summer migrations would be profited by a little judicious week-ending! How it would disorganize their factions and rearrange their prejudices! It would recharge their spiritual batteries and air out the cupboards of their souls. It would set local rivalries in a more tolerant perspective, and ease the cruel friction of rural life, which is so real to them and to us migrants so like a stage play. An occasional holiday on London Bridge, or its American equivalent, might send them home again with eyes to find the pot of gold under the tree in their backside.

Yet much week-ending might blur the piquant outlines of personality, dull imagination, and conventionalize speech. The other day, as we were gathering minnows from a creek, the forester's boys came down the road. With bucolic courtesy we asked where they were going. They answered without emotion that they were after their colt: "The blame shrimp swum the lake." Mark the passionless restraint of the reproach, and the fine propriety of the figure. From the hotel-keeper, who is our local eponym, we later learned the climax of the colt's exploits. The spirited creature had effected a landing at the hotel, and seizing the bell-rope in his teeth, had roused the slumbering establishment with wild alarm. Even a colt will have his holiday on London Bridge, and if there is no bridge where one should be, will swim for it perforce. So deep is the week-ending instinct.

On a peaceful evening, summer before last,

the semi-weekly freight brought a certain long-expected launch; and as the next day was the Fourth of July, it seemed very necessary to get the boat into the water that night. Half the men of our village had been retained to help in this, and a boat-wagon, especially designed for such ceremonies, was in attendance. The locomotive obligingly left the car with its end to the road, so that the boat might be shoved from its fastenings upon the wagon, and the waiting cohort immediately swarmed over car and launch, tearing off crating, wrenching away supports, and heaving the hull laboriously out of its cradle.

The other half of the villagers looked on and helped with interested advice. Among them appeared one of our neighbors, a veritable Captain of Industry, who had come down to the train to meet a cow. Instinctively he took command, and instinctively we all obeyed. It almost restored one's faith in the industrial order. "Here, Bill! get your back into this," he cried to the mightiest of the onlookers. Bill only wanted to be called on. He sprang upon the car, his brothers close behind him. The scene became Homeric. The car was thick with straining men. There was a clamor of voices. The horses became frightened and had to be taken from the wagon. A judge of the state Supreme Court sprang in to take their place, and held the tongue. What an allegory! Justice Holding the Tongue of Transportation! The Captain of Industry moved about, adjusting the packing and giving crisp directions. The twilight faded, and night was falling. At length, a final heave, and the hull slid down upon the wagon. The supreme justice was relieved, the horses were put in, the preferred half of the villagers scrambled upon the hull, and as the wagon creaked away toward the lake and the moon mounted above the pines, we dispersed with a friendlier understanding for a half-hour's common toil.

Sometimes, of a Saturday night, the transient and the permanent elements of our sparse population meet for a dance at the so-called rink. The big, bare room is dimly lighted with a few oil-lamps, and in the corner the burly forest-ranger, with his fiddle, leads the orchestral trio. The station agent, the inexorable custodian of our telegrams and express parcels, attends thinly disguised as a German peasant, and all make a diligent show of enjoyment. For this is a truly decorous affair, and you may find more real gaiety at many a prayer-meeting. The music belongs to the epoch of the waltz, and the Virginia Reel and the old reliable Lancers are seen again. Then, before the hour of midnight checks the patriot's use of pleasure gas, we scatter to our Fords and launches, and speed homeward under a glorious autumn aurora, just like the picture in the dictionary.

My week-ending will run into some six thousand miles this summer, and as Stevenson says of voyaging in the South Seas, it seems strange to travel so far and see so little. But what people one meets and what narratives one hears! Once in a while you may encounter that rare old species of raconteur, the Lion of the Smoking-Room. As

soon as he begins to talk, that luxurious retreat quickly fills up with an attentive group.

It was from a superb specimen of this van-
ishing race that I heard the legend of the
Camels of Arizona. It would seem that long
ago, before the Civil War, when Jefferson
Davis was Secretary of War, it was observed
that the Government Mule was not adapted
to use on the American Desert. The resourceful strategists of that epoch bethought them
of the oriental camel, the Ship of the Desert,
and the War Department accordingly imported a number of these animals to carry
supplies and ammunition to the waterless
parts of the West. This picturesque experiment was not, however, successful. The
loads were too heavy; the camels were less
amenable to military discipline than their
pictures had led Mr. Davis to suppose; and
a rapprochement between them and the
mule-drivers proved difficult to effect. At all
events, the stately creatures soon died or deserted, and the military phase of the experiment was over. But on clear nights, more

[211]

especially after pay-day, the belated rancher has often seen the weird forms of them or their posterity, swinging off across the moonlit sands among the mesas.

I have not been able to substantiate this legend in any particular, and I shudder to think what a wreck historical criticism might make of it. It is not as fact that it interests me, but as imagination; as the finest example I know of the Smoking-Room Legend; or, shall we say, the Pipe Dream?

In my adventurous youth, I stood one evening on the Wielandshöhe overlooking the river Neckar and the little city of Tübingen. It was a peaceful scene. Far below me a cavalcade of students, booted and spurred, rode two and two across the bridge to some distant rendezvous among the hills. Suddenly, around a bend in the river there swept into view a long raft of logs, steered down the swift stream by a little crew of lumbermen, on its way from the Black Forest to the Rhine. Instantly in all the Verein-houses that crowned the heights, windows were thrown up, heads were thrust out, and a chorus of hoots and cries filled the evening air. One corps vied with another in shouting derision at the little band of raftsmen, and the storm of sound pursued them until the raft disappeared from sight behind a hill below the town, when the uproar ceased as suddenly as it had begun.

So does the cloistered student, like the London shopman, cry out in mingled envy and derision upon the free adventurer in his quest for the pot of gold which is the week-ender's exceeding great reward.

PERSONS AND THINGS

PRACTICAL people are constantly telling us to look facts in the face, and to see things as they are. They would have us focus our attention upon the realities of life and act accordingly. This is well; but it is quite as important to bear in mind that this is not simply a world of fact and reality, but something rather more intricate and interesting, in which persons are often as important as things, and feelings, as facts. It is perhaps sad that we must allow for sentiment, but the truth is most people suffer from it in some form or other, and their giving and even their buying will be to some extent affected by it.

We live in an age that is all but overwhelmed by a flood of new facts, and old facts seen in new lights, and both of these everyone should welcome. Science and history have given them to us in an amazing measure, and yet they have evidently only begun. We shall be periodically inundated with new bodies of fact, at least for a long time to come. And this should be a veritable gospel for mankind. What better news could we have than that new fountains of information are opening to the human mind, to better our lot and clarify our vision? I would not, for a moment, be one of those who would turn away from this new knowledge with doubt or disdain.

What does need to be said, however, in the presence of much of it and the prospect of more is that facts are not everything. This flood of facts must not sweep us away from those values in personality and sentiment which are after all fundamental. The world still consists of people quite as much as things, and nothing has happened to make them really any more negligible than they ever were. Indeed, the importance of people seems in a fair way to be enhanced instead of being diminished by this new mastery of facts.

How it enlarges their sphere of influence for one thing! I remember with gratitude a certain plumber who when our radius rod broke in the Bad River Reservation generously replaced it with his own and sent us on our way rejoicing. He was, like us, from Chicago, and was just camping in the Indian village while he built himself a motor-boat to descend the Mississippi for a vacation. A most improbable situation, truly! Yet it is with just such improbabilities that the new age constantly confronts us, and I for one am in no mood to complain. What Indian of the Bad River could have done for me what that exotic Chicago plumber did? But what had brought him there? The gas engine, which was also to bear him thence. No, the individual need not wither while the world is more and more. He may expand, and fill the earth, meeting you this week on the Bad River and next week at Biloxi, or the Pass.

PERSONS AND THINGS

Doubtless plumbers are born for emergency; a young pupil of mine once defined plumbing as a set of pipes in need of repair. But the widened horizons of the new age are not theirs alone. A young man at a Christmas party offers to take your cousin home to Columbus in an airplane, with no more perturbation than you used to feel in inviting a girl to go bicycling; and off they float next day in a huge biplane and make Columbus in an hour and a half. Who says the individual withers? The poet was mistaken. The old Hebrews with their exultant forecast of man's dominion over nature were much nearer the truth.

All the more, then, are men and women to be reckoned with in making up the new account. The ancient, with no implement better than a hoe, might perhaps for purposes of argument be discounted. But the modern man who flies over the continent from sea to sea, looking down like an eagle into the Yellowstone, and the Yosemite, the Grand Canyon, and Death Valley, is certainly as important as the plane he flies in. And his character and ambitions, his hopes and fears, increase in importance with his powers.

What are we but bundles of experiences and acquisitions, sentiments and resolutions? And the more we have seen and felt and been and done, the more considerable bundles we become. It will be strange indeed if personality cannot keep pace with the advancing revelation of fact, however magnificent that revelation may be.

Not simply facts, things, and realities, then, but people, wishes, and sentiments must enter into all our serious practical estimates. In a remote village in South Dakota you will find a community-house with dining-room, kitchen, and assembly-room, and not far away a municipal swimming-pool, to evidence the spirit of the place. A like proportion of civic devotion would work wonders in many a bigger place much nearer the Atlantic Coast. You stopped there for a half-hour to mend a tire, and you found a shrine of pure democracy, with an enthusiastic citizen for its high priest.

People seem perfectly mobile, but they have a curious way of striking unseen roots into the soil. A young woman desiring to bring her parents from Sweden to America slaved and saved to get them here, only to find out that they could not bear the change and positively pined away until she sent them back to their native land. They were too old to transplant, and she had seen the change with her eyes instead of theirs. Some efforts to transplant institutions of learning have been just as promising and just as futile. What is really a good thing may be very bad for the actual people it would involve. It may seem very desirable to substitute the atmosphere of a factory for that of an office, until it occurs to one that people are involved, who may see the matter quite differently. Whether things are of more conse_ quence than persons may be disputed, but it is safe to say that the personal equation can never be entirely overlooked.

And yet many excellent men persist in acting as though they lived in a world of facts, realities, and things. Perpetually coming to grief on this theory, they mourn over the intractableness of the materials on which they imagine they are called to work. They have fallen into the way of thinking that everyone else belongs to the category of things for them to manipulate. They belong in an impersonal universe—a universe of things. What desolations they make in in the earth!

Yet the greatest loss is theirs, for they never become really conscious of the world they live in—in so far, at least, as they may be said to live in it. The better half of life, which is one's relations to persons, is closed to them. To think of all other persons as things carries with it its own sufficient penalty. What could be blanker than to go through life unconscious of all the people around you—their hopes, fears, and aspirations?

I would even go so far as to raise the question whether things have much of any value except in relation to persons—as desired, feared, acquired, used by them. Gold and diamonds, for example. Or oysters. A Sioux Indian of my acquaintance tells me that his first impressions on getting a raw oyster into his mouth were indescribable. He really did not know what to do with it. Yet Sioux and oysters have existed side by side on this continent for generations. But they had never met, and so the oyster had no value to the Sioux. Rude Africans who part with rough diamonds for a trifle are making no mistake. They cannot grind or set them, or wear them to the opera, and they find more use and enjoyment in a piece of calico or a handful of beads than in the white pebbles which the white man so prizes. But the white man has no use for them; he must pass them on from hand to hand until they reach the select and limited group which values them. It may be otherwise far away in the interstellar spaces, but among mankind things take their value from what man or woman can do with them. And this, in turn, depends very largely upon the degree of development of man or woman.

A gentleman with a good salable article called upon a dealer to stock up with it. "I will," replied the dealer, "provided you will first go out into my territory and create a demand for it." It was a good article, but that was not enough. People had to be shown this. Its own mere excellence would not alone sell it. So constantly are we brought back to people—their wants, real or imaginary, their desires and attitudes. This is what makes markets, literatures, cults, and politics. To find the truth is not enough. We must persuade men, or the truth will slip back into the obscurity from which we have dragged it. It is not enough that it has worth; we must make people see the worth of it. Hence the deluge of advertisements that smothers us. They are one vast testimonial to the necessity of persuading people of the worth of things.

It remains to consider those extraordinary

beings who think they understand people in general, although unable to make anything of them in particular; who cannot get on with their wives or their office force, but feel competent to expound the art of living to the world at large. They may be politicians, preachers, editors, educators, or even essayists; but if they cannot succeed in the small, how can they expect to achieve the great? Yet there are many people who think that there is some essential difference between dealing with a few persons and with a great many persons, and even that failure with the few promises success with the many. They have indeed learned that the beings immediately around them are persons, but they still cling to the idea that the remoter circles of mankind are only things.

Journeying once through South Dakota we spent a night at a ranchhouse, and in the evening sat in front of it and held converse with the rancher and his neighbors, who had been helping him with his threshing. Their talk, shrewd, humorous, practical, kindly, at once peopled those great plains for us with men and women not at all unlike ourselves, except that they were perhaps busier, pluckier, and more indomitable. Since when, the idle table-talk of cities and of newspapers about Dakota and its people sets us smiling to remember that night under the western stars.

And in a small town in Montana, in a restaurant so well kept that it surprises you in a land of individual platter service and unforgettable "merchant's lunches," you fall into conversation with the proprietor and learn what men like him have been through in recent years, with prolonged winters, dry summers, crop failures, bank failures, and all the ruinous adjustments in their wake; and how he had contrived to save his ranch and some cattle, and becoming possessed of a small restaurant in the town had seen how to combine the two and make a living. That story of the failure of the short grass so necessary in Montana grazing, and of what came of it, was a little epic of western hardship and courage. The world is certainly full of people, and a great many of them are great people, too.

Not a few excellent people feel the direst misgivings about the world of humanity beyond their immediate ken. In their own kind of people they feel the greatest satisfaction and confidence, but of all other kinds they are ready to despair. As they reflect upon the indolence, improvidence, extravagance, and decadence of artisans, laborers, and most wage-earners, a settled melancholy possesses them. They sincerely believe that all such people squander their leisure and their substance, and that high wages and short hours are worse than wasted on them. These gloomy spirits are laboring under the old delusion that this is a world of things, and that things are worth more than people.

So with all our flooding tide of facts and things, we may find comfort in the reflection that man has not yet, like Frankenstein, produced his dreaded master, but remains, for the present at least, a bigger thing than all his cinemas and phonographs, yes, even than his airplanes and radios; indeed all the bigger perhaps for having made them.